The EZ Big Book of
Alcoholics Anonymous

The EZ Big Book
of
Alcoholics Anonymous

SAME MESSAGE—
SIMPLE LANGUAGE

By a Member of A.A.

©2015 BeaconStreetUSA
Gainesville, Florida, USA
http://www.BeaconStreetUSA.com

BeaconStreetUSA, Publisher
5429 SW 80 Street
Gainesville, FL 32608

ISBN 0692397450
ISBN 13: 9780692397459

Printed in the United States of America

To Bill Wilson,
who created a vision for us.

"A.A. must and will continue to change with the passing years. We cannot, nor should we, turn back the clock."

--From Bill Wilson's last message to AA, 1970

Preface

—

History of AA's Big Book

IN 1939, BILL WILSON, COFOUNDER of AA, wrote a twelve-step guidebook for recovering alcoholics titled *Alcoholics Anonymous*. His 164-page text, usually referred to as the *Big Book*, described a program that helped him and other alcoholics give up liquor for good.

The earliest AA members were mostly professional men whose lives had almost been destroyed by drinking alcohol. Desperate for a cure, they had tried everything. Then they created a spiritual program of recovery that included practical action steps.

Big Book sales were slow until 1939, when *Liberty* magazine published an article about AA titled "Alcoholics and God." *Liberty* readers deluged the little AA office in New York with inquiries.

Two years later, a feature article about AA appeared in the *Saturday Evening Post*. The description of AA's successes was so convincing that the New York AA office was again flooded with requests for the book.

As the fellowship became more widely known, it grew. By 1976, the book had sold over one million copies, and there were over a million AA members worldwide. Since 1939, *Alcoholics Anonymous* has gone through more than sixty printings. For over six decades, few changes have been made in the basic text.

Foreword

Author's Note

SOME AA MEMBERS FIND BILL Wilson's original text, *Alcoholics Anonymous*, difficult to read. It was written in the 1930s for mainly college-level readers. Most were family men with stay-at-home wives. Their spiritual path was usually Christian. Obviously, lifestyles have changed since then.

The *EZ Big Book of Alcoholics Anonymous* is written in simple, straightforward English. The text is gender-neutral and encompasses a variety of lifestyles and spiritual paths. The book is a paragraph-by-paragraph editorial revision of Bill Wilson's original text.

Contents

Introduction

———

The Doctor's Opinion

As a reader wanting to know more about alcoholism, you might be interested in doctors' opinions of the spiritual program of Alcoholics Anonymous. They have watched many suffering alcoholics follow the plan outlined in this book and return to good health.

Dr. William Silkworth, well-known director of a famous hospital for alcoholics and addicts in the 1930s, wrote a letter to AA about the effects of the program on his patients.

He gave an example of a man who'd had a successful career but was ruining his life with drinking. At first the doctor considered his alcoholism hopeless. But then he saw the man give up alcohol by means of a new method.

After several visits, the man asked the doctor's permission to talk to other alcoholic patients about his method. His idea was that if they managed to recover, they could carry the AA message and help even more suffering drinkers.

Seeing the encouraging results of the man's effort, Dr. Silkworth predicted that this movement would grow and would open a new era of hope for alcoholics. At the time the doctor wrote his letter, the AA fellowship had over 100 recovering alcoholics.

Dr. Silkworth believed what AA's founders and other early members of the program already knew that the bodies of alcoholics are as sick as their minds. It does no good to point out their failure to adjust to life, to tell them they're trying to escape reality, or to warn them that they may be mentally ill, although that's certainly true of many.

Dr. Silkworth held the theory that alcoholics have an allergy to alcohol. Bill Wilson and other early members of AA thought he was right. It explained many aspects of their drinking problem.

After reading the book *Alcoholics Anonymous*, Dr. Silkworth recommended it to his patients. He said that, although physicians realize that alcoholics need moral help, they don't know how to give it. It's outside their medical knowledge.

It was Bill Wilson's opinion that some alcoholics require more than spiritual guidance as they begin recovery. Hospitalization or time in a treatment center may be needed to clear their brains so they can better understand what AA has to offer.

When asked by the author to write a statement for this book, Dr. Silkworth gladly complied. He believed in the ideas covered "in such masterly detail." He admitted that the moral psychology needed by alcoholics to recover was beyond the reach of most doctors. He wrote, "What with our ultra-modern standards, our scientific approach to everything, we are perhaps not well equipped to apply the powers of good that lie outside our synthetic knowledge."

In his statement, Dr. Silkworth referred to a patient who had once stayed in his hospital and wanted to carry the AA message to inpatient alcoholics. At first, the staff hesitated. Soon, though, the effects of the program amazed them. Members of the fellowship were unselfish, generous, and wanted no money for their services. They all believed that some kind of Higher Power had pulled them back from certain death.

The craving for alcohol doesn't always go away quickly, Dr. Silkworth observed. Once alcoholics have the drinking habit, they may not be able to break it. Their problems keep getting worse. It's a symptom of an allergy to alcohol that is never seen in normal drinkers. This is where hospital treatment helps. Eventually, though, alcoholics must put their trust in a power greater than themselves.

Dr. Silkworth described the ravages of alcoholism that he and other psychiatrists witnessed every day. The effects of the disease left husbands, wives, and children in despair. Many alcoholics seemed to be past all help. Dr. Silkworth agreed with the AA principle that hope must come from belief in a Higher Power if an alcoholic expects to recover.

In Dr. Silkworth's experience, the AA program did what physicians could not. To any doubting professionals, he suggested that they try to help solve the alcoholic's problems as part of their daily work. Then, he said, they will understand why he and his colleagues support the movement. He wrote that nothing contributes more to the recovery of alcoholics than the unselfish fellowship growing among them.

Dr. Silkworth explained that alcoholics drink for the feeling it gives them. Even after their drinking has started causing problems, they think their life is normal. Without liquor inside them, they feel restless, irritable, and discontented. Drinking brings them a sense of comfort and ease. They think, "Why shouldn't I be able to drink like other people do?"

Dr. Silkworth described the cycle that alcoholics go through. After they've managed to quit drinking for a while, they surrender to the craving for alcohol. They go on a spree. When it's over, they feel guilty. They promise never to do it again. But they do.

Unless they have an entire psychic change of the kind described in the book *Alcoholics Anonymous*, they have little hope of recovery. However, once this change occurs, alcoholics find their craving easy to control—but only if they abstain from liquor entirely.

Faced with patients who beg for rescue from their alcoholism, doctors often feel helpless. They can give their all, but it's seldom enough. Many sense that more than human aid is needed to cure the alcoholic.

Dr. Silkworth believed that willpower is not the answer. He treated many patients who had every reason to avoid alcohol. They risked losing successful careers if they picked up another drink. Yet when the craving hit them, they started again with no thought of the consequences.

The classification of alcoholics is difficult, Dr. Silkworth wrote. Some have psychiatric illness. These mentally unstable patients vow to quit forever, but soon go back to drinking and then show great remorse at every binge. Others won't admit that they are powerless over alcohol and try all sorts of strategies to control their drinking, such as switching brands of alcohol or changing the places where they drink. Others think they're cured after they've succeeded in quitting for a period of time.

Many alcoholics are normal in every respect other than the effect alcohol has on them. Alcoholics share one symptom. Once they take a drink, they crave more. The only cure is total avoidance of liquor.

One patient came to Dr. Silkworth after a bout of gastric bleeding. The man was going downhill mentally. He'd lost everything of value in life and lived only to drink. After alcohol was taken away, the doctors could find no lasting brain damage, and the man agreed to try the plan in this book.

A year later, the patient returned to visit Dr. Silkworth. The doctor thought the man looked familiar but couldn't place him. The man had gone from a hopeless, shaking wreck to a person filled with contentment. Even after their talk, Dr. Silkworth couldn't connect this visitor with the man he'd seen a year earlier. To the doctor's knowledge, the man never drank again.

Dr. Silkworth had another patient who recognized that he was an alcoholic and had no hope for the future. The man hid in an empty barn and waited to die. A search party found him and brought him to the hospital in desperate condition.

The patient told Dr. Silkworth that treatment would be a waste of effort unless it would give him the willpower to resist alcohol. The man was admitted to the hospital even though the doctors saw little hope. There, the man became sold on the ideas in the book *Alcoholics Anonymous* and never drank again. In the doctor's words, "He is as fine a man as one could wish to meet."

Dr. Silkworth ended his letter with these words: "I sincerely advise every alcoholic to read this book through, and though perhaps he came to scoff, he may remain to pray."

Chapter 1

———

Bill's Story

DURING WORLD WAR I, BILL Wilson was a young army officer stationed in Plattsburgh, New York. The local people welcomed Bill and his fellow officers into their homes, treating them like heroes. In the midst of the excitement, Bill discovered liquor, forgetting his family's warnings about the dangers of drinking.

After shipping overseas, Bill turned to alcohol when he got lonely. While in England, he visited an ancient cathedral and walked around the cemetery outside. He noticed a verse on an old tombstone, but ignored its warning:

Here lies a Hampshire Grenadier
Who caught his death
Drinking cold small beer
A good soldier is ne'er forgot
Whether he dieth by musket *[gun]*
Or by pot *[large cup]*

Bill was 22 when the war ended. Returning home, he was proud of his leadership record in the army and knew he was destined for great things. He got a job and studied law at night, but his drinking interfered with his studying so he almost flunked his first exam. He was too drunk to think or write.

Still, he was sure he'd succeed. His job took him to Wall Street, where he watched people get rich on the stock market. "Why not me?" he thought.

Bill's drinking worried his wife. When they had discussions about it, he assured her that the world's geniuses thought up their greatest ideas while drinking.

Bill knew that law practice was not for him, but he loved Wall Street. Financial leaders were his heroes. Between gambling on the stock market and drinking, he had carved a boomerang that, in his words, "later turned on me and almost cut me to pieces."

Bill and his wife managed to save a thousand dollars by living carefully. He used part of the money to buy cheap securities on the stock market and waited for their price to rise. When he couldn't persuade his broker friends to send him out looking for business, Bill and his wife went on their own. Bill's theory was that people lost money in the stock market because of ignorance. Later, he found more reasons.

The couple roared out of town on a motorcycle. The sidecar was stuffed with a tent, blankets, clothes, and books about finance. Their friends thought they were crazy.

Because Bill had some success on the stock market, they had a little money. Once, though, they had to work on a farm for a month. Bill wrote, "That was my last honest work for a long time."

In the next year, they covered the eastern United States. Finally, he landed a job with an expense account on Wall Street. With more money coming in from stocks, he put away several thousand dollars.

The next few years were lucky. Bill made money and gained a good reputation. In the financial boom of the late 1920s, his profits amounted to millions of dollars—on paper, at least.

Alcohol was becoming more important in Bill's life. He made fair-weather friends in the New York nightclubs. The bars were packed with excited people spending money by the thousands and talking in the millions. Before long, Bill was drinking all day and most nights.

When friends warned him about his drinking, Bill got defensive. Soon he became a lone wolf. He had arguments with his wife. At least he could claim that he didn't get involved with women. "I didn't have affairs because I was loyal to my wife—and maybe too drunk."

In 1929, Bill caught golf fever. He and his wife moved to the country, and soon he was playing like a pro. He loved playing on the rich folks' golf courses that impressed him so much as a boy. The sport allowed him to drink day and night. He bought expensive tailored clothes and acquired a great tan. He wrote fat checks while his banker looked on with doubt.

Soon liquor caught up with Bill. At the same time, hell broke loose on the New York Stock Exchange. One night in October 1929, he staggered from a bar to a broker's office after the market closed. One of his stocks had dropped from 52 to 32 that day.

The newspapers reported men jumping to their deaths from office windows. Bill's friends had lost millions since morning. "So what?" he thought. "Tomorrow is another day." As he drank, his old will to win came back.

The next day, he phoned a friend in Canada who still had money. Bill and his wife moved to Montreal and started living in style again. Before long, though, Bill's drinking got so bad that his generous friend had to let him go. After that, the couple stayed broke.

They went to live with his wife's parents. Bill found a job but soon lost it as the result of a fight. No one knew then that he'd be out of work and hardly draw a sober breath for five years.

His wife took a job in a department store. Coming home worn out at night, she'd find Bill drunk. He tried to visit Wall Street offices, but he was no longer welcome there.

Now liquor was no longer a luxury. Bill had to have it. It was routine for him to drink two or three bottles of bootleg gin a day. Sometimes he'd make a few hundred dollars on a business deal, enough to pay his bills at the bars and delis.

This went on and on. He started waking up early in the morning with the shakes. He needed a glass of gin and several beers before he could eat breakfast. Still, he convinced himself that he was in control. He even had sober spells that gave his wife new hope.

Things got worse. The bank foreclosed on their mortgage. His mother-in-law died, and both his wife and father-in-law got sick.

In 1932, when stocks were at a low point, Bill had a lucky break. He was able to form a group of buyers for an investment, and he expected a big share of the profits. But he got drunk and the chance slipped away.

Writing about that period of his life, Bill recalled that he knew he had to stop. He couldn't take even one drink. He swore to quit for good. He'd promised before, but this time his wife believed him.

He came home drunk again, without even resisting the alcohol. He had no idea what happened. Someone pushed a drink his way and he took it. Such a terrible lack of judgment made him wonder if he was crazy.

Bill vowed to try again. He did so well that he went from being confident to turning cocky. "I could laugh at booze," he said. "I thought I had what it takes."

One day he went into a restaurant to make a phone call. In no time, he was pounding on the bar with a whiskey in his hand, asking himself what happened. As the alcohol started taking effect, he figured he might as well go ahead and get drunk. He'd do better next time.

The next morning, his courage was gone and he felt doomed. He was afraid to cross the street because he might fall down and get run over by a truck. It was dawn when he went out, and an all-night place gave him a dozen glasses of ale to quiet his nerves.

In the morning paper, he saw that the market had gone to hell again. "Well, so have I," he thought. The market would come back, but he wouldn't. He considered killing himself, but decided to have some gin instead. He drank two bottles and blacked out.

Bill's body endured this for two more years. Sometimes he stole money from his wife's purse to buy booze so he could calm the morning jitters. He considered jumping out of their apartment window many stories up or taking poison from the medicine chest. But then he cursed himself for being weak.

One night, the torture was so bad he was sure he couldn't stop himself from jumping to his death. Somehow, he dragged his mattress to safety on a lower floor. A doctor was called and gave him a sedative. The next day, Bill added gin to the sedative and was in worse shape than ever.

People feared that he was losing his mind. So did Bill. He ate almost nothing when drinking and was 40 pounds underweight.

His brother-in-law, a physician, offered to get Bill admitted to a famous treatment center. After taking medications for withdrawal, undergoing a course of physical therapy, and getting some exercise, his mind cleared. A doctor explained that while Bill was certainly selfish and foolish, he was also seriously ill.

Bill was relieved to learn that an alcoholic's willpower is terribly weak when it comes to liquor, no matter how strong it is in other ways. This explained why he couldn't stop drinking even though he desperately wanted to. Bill said, "Now that I knew myself better, I had hope."

For a few months, things went great. He went to town often and made a little money. He thought that self-knowledge was surely the key.

But the awful day came when he drank again. His spirits and his health hit a new low. So he returned to the hospital.

He thought he'd come to the end. The doctors told his desperate wife that Bill would probably die of heart failure or have brain damage within a year. She'd have to turn him over to a mental hospital or an undertaker.

Bill almost welcomed the idea, despite the blow to his pride. He had always thought well of himself and his ability to overcome his troubles. But now he was about to fall into a dark pit, joining all the drunks who went before him.

He thought of the happy life he'd had with his wife. That was over. He'd give anything to make amends. His self-pity was enormous. Alcohol was his master.

Bill left the hospital a broken man. Fear kept him sober for a while, but the insanity returned on Veteran's Day, 1934. He was off again. Everyone accepted the fact that Bill would either have to be locked up or he'd stumble along to a tragic end.

Bill wrote, "How dark it is before the dawn! Actually, I was near my last drunk. I was soon to enter a life of happiness, peace, and usefulness—a life that has become more wonderful as time passes."

One afternoon that November, he was drinking at his kitchen table while his wife was at work. He was glad he'd hidden enough gin around the house to last through the night and the next day. He thought about hiding a full bottle near the head of the bed because he knew he'd need it before dawn.

The phone rang. On the other end of the line was the happy voice of an old school friend who wanted to come and visit. He was sober! It was years since Bill could remember his friend coming to New York without drinking. Bill had heard that the friend had been locked up for alcoholic insanity, and Bill wondered how he'd escaped.

Bill planned to enjoy an evening of drinking together. He remembered the fun of the old days, like the time they chartered a plane while drunk. The friend's arrival in town was an oasis in the desert of Bill's life.

When the friend arrived, his skin was healthy and glowing. His eyes had a new look. Bill wondered what had happened, but pushed a drink toward his friend. The friend refused it!

"What's this all about?" Bill asked.

The friend smiled. "I've got religion."

Bill was shocked. He thought, "Last summer he was an alcoholic nut. Now he's a religious nut … well, bless his heart, let him talk. My gin will last longer than his preaching."

But the friend didn't preach. He told a story about two men who appeared in court for him and talked the judge into suspending his sentence. They told him about a simple spiritual idea and program of action. Obviously, it had worked.

The friend wanted to tell Bill about it. They talked for hours, recalling childhood memories. As they sat there, Bill recollected his preacher's voice on Sundays, giving him the chance to take an abstinence pledge. He never did. Bill remembered how his grandfather looked down on church people and figured the preacher had no right to tell him how to live.

Bill always believed in a Power greater than himself. He was not an atheist who took the view that the universe came from nowhere and is going nowhere. Scientists, his heroes, suggested that great forces were at work. Bill believed that a purpose was behind everything, but that was as far as he'd gone.

He'd turned away from religion and was irritated by talk of a "personal God of love." He considered that Christ was a great man, but Christians didn't follow his teachings very well. Bill said, "I myself used the parts that were convenient and not too hard. The rest I ignored."

Human cruelty throughout history made him sick, and he couldn't see that religion had done the world much good. He considered the "brotherhood of man" a joke. In his opinion, the Devil, if there was one, was probably the real boss of things.

But his friend sat there and insisted that God had done for him what he couldn't do for himself. His will had failed him entirely. His doctors gave him no hope for a cure and were ready to lock him up. Then his newfound faith lifted him from the scrap heap of humanity to a life better than any he'd ever known.

Bill wondered whether this power had come from inside his friend. Obviously not. Bill wrote, "There was no more power in him than there was in me at that minute. And that was none at all."

Right then Bill threw out his old ideas about religion and miracles. He saw that his friend had totally changed and his roots had found new soil.

Still, Bill disliked the word "God." He rejected the idea of a personal God. He could accept a "Universal Spirit" but not a "King of Heaven."

His friend asked, "Why don't you choose a God of your own understanding?"

Bill said that those words melted his hardened beliefs of many years. He needed only to believe in a Power greater than himself to make a start. He could build a new foundation on this willingness. As his pride and prejudice fell away, a new world opened to him.

The real importance of his experience in the cemetery outside the English cathedral became clear. For a brief time, he'd needed and wanted a Higher Power, and it had come to him. But soon the noise of the world had blotted it out.

Shortly after his friend's visit, Bill entered the hospital. He'd had his last drink. Humbly asking for God's care and direction, he faced his past wrongdoings and became willing to make things right.

When Bill's old friend came to see him again, Bill talked about his faults and problems. Together they made a list of people Bill had harmed or whom he resented. Bill became willing to make amends to them any way he could.

He was told he could get a better sense of his Higher Power by sitting quietly when troubled and asking for the strength to solve his problems as God would want. He was to request nothing for himself except to be shown how he could be useful to others.

Bill's friend promised that if he did this, he would enter a new relationship with his Higher Power and discover a way of living that would solve all his problems. But it was essential for him to be honest, willing, and humble. However, there was a price. Bill had to give up being so self-centered. He had to turn in all things to a Higher Power.

While these ideas seemed drastic, the effect was amazing. Bill had a sense of victory, followed by peace, serenity, and confidence. He felt as though the clean wind of a mountaintop had blown through him. Accepting a Higher Power comes to most people gradually, he said, but the effect on him was sudden and deep.

These new feelings were so strong they scared Bill. His doctor said, "Something has happened to you that I don't understand. But you'd better hang onto it. Anything is better than the way you were."

While Bill was in the hospital, it occurred to him that thousands of other hopeless alcoholics might benefit from what was so freely given to him. If he could help them, they could go on to help others.

Bill's friend made clear the need to practice these principles in all his affairs. He emphasized that faith without works is dead. If alcoholics don't expand their spiritual lives through work and self-sacrifice, they can't survive the low points ahead, the friend said. They'll drink again. And if they drink, they'll die.

Bill and his wife devoted themselves to helping other alcoholics. He had plenty of free time because his old business friends hesitated to give him work. Although he wasn't well at the time and suffered waves of self-pity and resentment, working with others saved him every time. Reaching out to alcoholics at the hospital always lifted him up.

Bill and his wife began to make close friends in the AA fellowship, finding joy in their lives even when times were rough. They watched families solve problems that seemed impossible. Bitterness of the past was wiped out.

Bill saw alcoholics leave mental hospitals to take up vital roles in their families and communities. The reputations of professional people were restored. The AA program helped newcomers overcome every kind of trouble.

Bill observed, "Active alcoholics are not attractive people. Our struggles with them can be difficult and sad. One poor man committed suicide in my home."

There's fun in it, too, Bill pointed out. Outsiders might be shocked at the liveliness and humor of recovering alcoholics. But under it all, they're deadly serious.

Bill was convinced that most alcoholics need to look no further for heaven. "We have it with us right here and now."

Chapter 2

－－－

There Is a Solution

Many of us in AA were as hopeless as Bill W. before we stopped drinking. Our fellowship consists of average people of many backgrounds. Normally, we would never meet. But in AA, we enjoy an amazing closeness. We're like survivors of a shipwreck.

In AA groups, we're connected by friendship and equality because we've found a common solution to our problems. Even as we go our individual ways in life, the feeling of being rescued from the same peril binds us together. We have a way out that we all agree on.

The disease of alcoholism takes its toll on people around the alcoholic in a way no other does. The family of a person with cancer is upset, but they're not hurt or angry with the patient. This isn't true of the family of the alcoholic and all the other people whose lives are damaged by the drinker.

Alcoholism frustrates employers, brings financial disaster to drinkers and their families, and causes resentments all around. It creates havoc in the lives of relatives and friends. We hope this book will help and comfort the families of alcoholics, as well as the alcoholics themselves.

The best psychiatrists often can't get alcoholics to talk about their problem. The same is true of their partners, parents, and friends. But usually one alcoholic can get another to open up within a few hours. This kind of understanding is essential for an alcoholic to move forward in recovery.

People in AA know what they're talking about. Their whole manner shows that they have a solution. They're not trying to be better than the next person or give lectures. They don't expect people to please them and won't take money. They simply have a sincere desire to help. When such people reach out to a practicing alcoholic, the person can start on the road to recovery.

As members of AA, we don't make a full-time job of helping other alcoholics. In fact, it wouldn't make us more effective. Many of us devote much of our spare time to this effort, however. We reach out to those still suffering from the disease and show them how to apply the principles of AA at home, at work, and in all their affairs.

If AA continues this work, our communities are bound to benefit. Still, we can barely scratch the surface. In big cities, hundreds of alcoholics drop out of sight each day. Given the chance, many of them could get well. It's our aim to share what's been so freely given to us.

This book describes our experience and the AA program of action. Recovering alcoholics know that their lives depend on concern for others and making an effort to meet their needs.

In this book, we will discuss the medical and psychiatric aspects of alcoholism, as well as social and spiritual issues related to the disease. We have tried to approach sensitive topics with care, because people are more able to accept help when their views and opinions are respected.

You may wonder how alcoholics become so damaged from drinking. How can they recover from a disease that experts consider almost impossible to treat? If you are an alcoholic who wants to give up liquor, you may be asking, "What do I have to do?"

This book explains the progressive nature of untreated alcoholism. It tells how AA members escaped their hopeless state of mind and body. If you have a problem with alcohol, the book tells you what you have to do to recover.

When we were still drinking, friends said things like, "I can take alcohol or leave it alone. Why can't you?" Or they asked, "If you can't drink like a normal person, why don't you quit?" Some suggested that we give up hard liquor and switch to beer or wine. Or they worked on our sense of guilt with comments like, "You've got such a great family. Can't you stop for their sake?"

These questions reflect a lack of understanding of the disease. Moderate drinkers can usually quit with no trouble if they have a good reason. This is even true of some hard drinkers. They may injure their health and even die a few years before their time. But if they have an illness that worsens with drinking or their doctor gives them a warning, they can manage to cut back or quit.

Real alcoholics are another story. They may start by drinking in moderation. But after a while they go much further. They lose control as soon as they swallow the first drink.

Their lack of control is a puzzle to outsiders. Alcoholic drinkers seldom get just a little high. They go all the way, acting insane when drunk. They do outrageous things, even though they may be the best people in the world while sober.

Drinking turns them into repulsive, dangerous human beings.

They have a knack for getting drunk at the wrong times. They get loaded just before a major decision or important event. They may be responsible in other ways, but they become selfish, dishonest people when they drink. If they have a successful career and promising future, they pull it down by a crazy series of sprees.

Many alcoholics go to bed drunk enough to make a normal person sleep around the clock. But they're up early the next morning, looking for the liquor they hid the night before. They may have bottles stashed all over the house so they'll have spares in case someone tries to throw their supply down the sink.

As things get worse, many alcoholics start taking drugs to calm their nerves so they can go to work. But the day comes when they can't make it. They get drunk all over again.

Some alcoholics go to doctors who prescribe medications to help them taper off. At this point, they're likely to start showing up in hospitals and institutions. These are just a few of the scenarios that we see among alcoholics.

It's a mystery how they can know that one drink always leads to suffering and humiliation, and yet drink anyhow. What happened to the common sense and willpower most of them show in other matters?

Maybe we'll never have the answer. We do know that when alcoholics stop drinking for months and years, they act fairly normal. But as soon as they take any liquor into their systems, something happens to their bodies and minds that makes it impossible to stop. Any recovering alcoholic can vouch for this.

Because the first drink starts things off, it's logical that the problem begins in the mind. When asked why they drink, alcoholics give many reasons, but their explanations make no sense when you look at the awful results. Even when some of the excuses sound reasonable, they don't add up when you consider the havoc caused by each drinking spree. If you point this out, the alcoholic will laugh at you or get irritated and refuse to talk.

Alcoholics who can be truthful about the matter admit that they have no idea why they took the first drink. Or they give excuses but know in their hearts that they're confused. Sometimes they're obsessed with the idea that one day they'll beat the game. Other times, they suspect they're down for the count.

Those close to the alcoholic sense that something is wrong, but they hope the alcoholic will wake up one day with the willpower to quit. Sadly, this rarely happens, for the drinker has lost all control. At some point, the greatest desire to quit does no good. Usually this stage is reached before anyone suspects it.

Most alcoholics have lost the power of choice. They have no defense against the first drink. They forget the suffering and humiliation of a few days earlier. If they do remember, they vow that they'll act like normal people next time.

The consequences of trying to take just one drink are almost always the same. Disaster. But this fact doesn't enter the mind of the alcoholic. Or if it does, he or she vows to drink like a normal person.

Who would be stupid enough to put their hands on a hot stove after they've been burned over and over? Yet, when a drink is offered to the alcoholic, he or she thinks, "This time I won't get burned." Or the person doesn't think at all.

Many of us had this carefree attitude. Then after the third or fourth drink, we'd say, "God, how did I get started again?" This thought is followed by, "Well, I'll stop with the sixth drink." Or "Why stop now?"

Alcoholics who have reached this stage are usually past ordinary human help. Unless they're locked up, they may die or go insane, as many alcoholics have. They want to stop, but can't.

There is a solution. Few of us cared to look at ourselves closely. We didn't want to lower our pride or admit our faults. But we had no future if we continued as we were. Then we saw that the AA program worked for other problem drinkers.

When approached by a recovering alcoholic, we became willing to try the program's spiritual tools. As a result, we found a better way of life than we'd ever dreamed possible.

We've had spiritual experiences that have affected our lives deeply. Our attitudes toward others and toward God's universe have changed. A Higher Power has entered our hearts and lives and worked miracles. It has done for us what we could never do for ourselves.

If your alcoholism is as serious as ours was, there's no middle-of-the road solution. We'd passed the point of no return. We could either continue as we were, trying to blot out the awareness of our wasted lives, or accept spiritual help.

We knew a man who had good business ability and character but whose drinking was out of control. He'd gone from one mental institution to another. He even consulted the famous Dr. Carl

Jung in Europe. Although cure was doubtful, he finished treatment in healthy physical and mental condition. He thought he understood himself so well that he couldn't relapse. In a short time he was drunk. What happened?

Returning to Europe, he asked Dr. Jung why he couldn't recover. He was desperate to get his self-discipline back. He was clear and sensible about his other problems. Why couldn't he control his drinking?

The man begged Dr. Jung for the truth. The doctor was honest. He considered the man hopeless and thought he'd have to put himself in an institution or hire a bodyguard if he expected to live long.

But this man still lives and is free to go anywhere with no problem. He just needs to maintain a certain spiritual attitude.

Some alcoholic readers may think that spiritual help isn't necessary. Here is what Dr. Jung shared with his patient: "You have the mind of a chronic alcoholic. I've never seen one single case recover where that state of mind existed to the extent that it does in you."

The man felt as though the gates of hell had just closed on him. He asked, "Are there no exceptions?"

"Yes," said the doctor, "since early times." He explained that once in a while, alcoholics have vital spiritual experiences consisting of huge psychological changes. Ideas, emotions, and attitudes that once guided the alcoholic are suddenly set aside, and a completely new set takes over. Dr. Jung told the patient that he'd been trying to produce this change in him. His methods, he said, succeeded with many people, but never with an alcoholic like this man.

This relieved the patient, who told the doctor he was a religious person. However, his hopes fell when Dr. Jung told him that while religious faith is good, it doesn't offer the kind of spiritual experience required. This left the man discouraged. Then, shortly afterward, he had a spiritual awakening of the kind described in *Alcoholics Anonymous*, and he found his freedom.

As alcoholics, we were desperate, too, until we discovered a loving Higher Power. Then we were given a new life—a design for living that worked.

The psychologist Henry James, author of *The Varieties of Religious Experience*, described ways in which people discover a Higher Power. Certainly, there is more than one. People of all races, creeds, and colors believe they were created by a Higher Power. In our fellowship, there is no argument over matters of faith. Personal beliefs, even atheism, are no great obstacle to a spiritual experience. Each of us must decide our spiritual path for ourselves.

The next chapter describes alcoholism as we understand it, followed by a chapter written for agnostic and atheist believers. Later, the book gives directions for recovery.

Chapter 3

More About Alcoholism

MOST OF US WOULDN'T ADMIT we were alcoholics. We tried to prove we could drink like normal people. We had the idea that somehow, some day, we could enjoy drinking and suffer no ill effects. Many alcoholics chase this dream to the gates of insanity or death.

Admitting that we were alcoholics was the first step in recovery. We are men and women who have lost the ability to control our drinking and will never get it back. The short periods we went without liquor were followed by even more drinking and less control. Our failures confused and depressed us.

As alcoholics, we have a progressive illness. In the long run, we get worse, not better. We're like people who have lost their legs. They'll never grow new ones.

We tried every known cure, but our drinking only got worse. Doctors agree that no one can make a normal drinker out of an alcoholic. Scientists may one day find a cure, but they haven't yet.

Many alcoholics are convinced that they don't really have this disease. They try to prove it by experimenting with different ways to cut down their drinking. Our hats are off to any alcoholic who can do it. Heaven knows we've tried.

We've tried switching from hard liquor to beer or wine. We tried limiting our drinks, never drinking alone, and never drinking in the morning or at home. We kept liquor out of the house and never drank during the day. We allowed ourselves alcohol only at parties. We vowed to quit our jobs if we ever showed up drunk at work. We decided to get away on a trip, stay home, or take no trips at all. We tried getting more exercise and reading self-help books. We even offered to go into treatment. The list goes on.

If you think you might be an alcoholic, here's how to find out. Go to a bar, start drinking, and then try to stop suddenly. Do this more than once. You'll soon discover whether you're an alcoholic.

In our early drinking days, most of us might have stopped. The trouble is, few alcoholics have the desire to quit while there's time. There are exceptions, though.

We know of a man who, when young and successful, was going on drinking sprees. To cure his morning-after hangovers, he'd drink more liquor. He soon realized that he'd lost the ability to quit after the first drink. Alcohol would wreck his career. At the age of thirty, he decided to wait until he retired before touching another drop. He retired at the age of fifty-five after a happy and successful career.

Then he was trapped by a belief held by most alcoholics—that years of sobriety would allow him to drink normally. He got out his slippers and a bottle.

In two months, the man was in the hospital, confused and ashamed. When he got out, he tried controlled drinking but always wound up in a hospital bed again. He resolved to stop completely this time and couldn't. He underwent every kind of treatment with no success. A healthy man on the day he retired, he went to pieces quickly and was dead within four years.

There's a lesson here. Some alcoholics can go without liquor for many years, but when they start again they're just where they left off years earlier. We've seen it again and again. Once an alcoholic, always an alcoholic. Those who are sincere about quitting can't hang on to the idea that some day they will be able to drink safely. It won't happen.

Young drinkers may view this man as proof that they, too, can give up liquor based on their own willpower. They may think this, but few are likely to give it a serious try. And if they do, they probably won't succeed. We've seen young people become as powerless over alcohol as long-term drinkers in just a few years.

Getting addicted to alcohol doesn't necessarily take long. Drinkers who'd be insulted to be called alcoholics are often amazed to find they can't leave it alone. It's especially hard for young alcoholics to admit they have the disease.

Looking back, we see that we'd continued drinking for many years after we could have quit on the basis of willpower. If you're not sure whether you've entered the danger zone, try abstaining for one year. If you're an alcoholic, you probably can't do it.

Early in our drinking, some of us stayed sober for a year or so but later became serious drinkers. Most potential alcoholics can't resist alcohol for anything close to a year. They get drunk within a few weeks.

If you can't drink in moderation, how do you stop completely? Whether it's possible without the aid of a spiritual program depends on how much you've lost the power to choose.

Many of us felt we had strength of character as well as a sincere desire to quit for good. Yet we couldn't leave liquor alone no matter how much we wanted to.

Trying to quit for a time will help you decide whether you're an alcoholic, but you should also be aware of the mental states that come before a relapse. What's wrong with the mind of the alcoholic who has tried many times to stop after the first drink and failed? Friends are astounded when the person whose life has been severely damaged by alcohol walks straight into a bar.

A friend we'll call Jim had a wonderful wife and family and owned a car dealership. He was intelligent, had a good military record, and people liked him. He seemed normal, although nervous. He didn't drink until age thirty-five. In a few years, he got so violent when drunk that he had to be hospitalized.

After discharge, he joined AA. He got his family back and took a sales job for the dealership he'd lost because of his drinking. He did fine for a while but failed to develop a spiritual approach to life. Then he got drunk several times in a row. Each time, we sat down with him and reviewed what had happened. He knew he was in bad shape and likely to lose the family he loved.

Still, he got drunk again. He explained that when he went to work that day, he was irritated that he had to work for a business he once owned. He had words with his boss, but nothing serious. Then he decided to drive to the country to see a man interested in a car.

On the way, he was hungry, so he stopped at a roadside diner with a bar. He had no thought of drinking. He just planned to get a sandwich. He also hoped he might find a customer at this place, where he'd gone for years. He ordered a glass of milk with his food. Still hungry, he ordered more food and milk.

Suddenly it occurred to him that adding an ounce of whiskey to the milk couldn't hurt him on a full stomach. He knew this wasn't too smart, but felt okay because he was taking the whiskey with food. This went so well he ordered another whiskey and poured it in. That didn't bother him either, so he tried another.

Jim ended up in the hospital again, even though he was aware of the price he'd have to pay. He had long since accepted the fact that he was an alcoholic. But he ignored this in favor of the foolish notion that he could drink whiskey if he mixed it with milk. This kind of thinking certainly seems "insane," however you define the word.

Jim was not an extreme case. We all thought like this. Some twist of logic led us to come up with crazy excuses for that first drink. The next day we asked ourselves how it could have happened.

Some of us had a good reason to get drunk, we thought. We had to calm our nerves or deal with our anger, worry, depression, jealousy, and so on. When we picked up the first drink we thought nothing of the outcome, which was always worse than the problems that started it off.

We act as insane as a person obsessed with jay-walking. He gets a thrill out of running in front of cars. He enjoys this for a few years even though he's warned of the dangers. Up to this point, you might just call him a guy with weird ideas of fun.

Then his luck runs out, and he's hit a few times. Wouldn't you think he'd stop? He doesn't. Soon he's hit again and fractures his skull. After he leaves the hospital, a bus runs into him, breaking his arm. He vows to quit for good, but in a few weeks, he's back on the street and both legs are broken in another accident.

This continues for years, until he can't work, his wife leaves him, and people make fun of him. He tries to cure his obsession but can't. He even enters an institution. The day he's out, he runs in front of a fire truck, breaking his back. Wouldn't you call this crazy?

You may find this example far-fetched. But if you substitute "alcoholism" for "jaywalking," it fits alcoholics perfectly. No matter how smart we may be, we're strangely insane when it comes to liquor.

You may think, "That story doesn't really apply to me. I haven't gone that far. I won't, either, now that I understand myself so well. I haven't lost everything through drinking and I don't plan to. Thanks for the information, though."

Some nonalcoholic drinkers who overdo liquor can stop or cut down when there's a good reason if their brains and bodies haven't been damaged as ours were. But few real alcoholics can give up liquor based on self-knowledge. We've learned this from bitter experience.

Fred is another example. As a partner in a large accounting firm, he earns a good income. He's happily married, lives in a beautiful home, and has intelligent children of college age. He makes friends easily. Fred appears to be well balanced, but he's an alcoholic.

We met him a year ago in a hospital. He had his first bad case of the jitters. Rather than admit he was an alcoholic, he said he was there to rest.

The doctor suggested that Fred might be worse than he thought. So Fred decided to quit drinking, never dreaming that he couldn't. He didn't believe he was an alcoholic and certainly wasn't interested in a spiritual cure.

He listened to our description of alcoholism and admitted he had some of the symptoms. But he thought he could solve the problem on his own. His feelings of shame plus what he'd learned from us would keep him sober the rest of his life, he thought.

After some time passed, we learned that Fred was back in the hospital, this time shaky and anxious to see us. He knew he had no excuse for drinking and had to stop. His judgment and will-power were good in other matters, but here he was, flat on his back again.

Fred admitted that he was impressed with what we had told him about alcoholism. He was sure it couldn't happen to him after what he'd learned. He'd solved his other personal difficulties and didn't think he was as far gone as most problem drinkers. It was only a matter of willpower and keeping his guard up.

One day, Fred went to Washington on busi-ness. He'd done this before when he was sober. He had no worries. His meeting went well, and he was pleased. He knew his partners would be, too. It was the end of a perfect day.

After dressing for dinner at the hotel and go-ing down to the dining room, he decided that a couple of cocktails would be nice. Nothing more. He ordered one with his meal. Then he ordered another.

After dinner, he took a walk. When he returned to the hotel, it struck him that a drink before bed would be good, so he went to the bar. He remembered having more that night and plenty the next morning.

When Fred returned home, his wife wasn't at the airport. A friendly cab driver drove him around town for several days. The next thing he knew, he was in the hospital again. After his mind cleared, he remembered that he started his drinking spree with no thought of the consequences. He drank cocktails as though they were ginger ale.

Fred recalled his friends' warnings—if he had an alcoholic mind, he would go back to drinking. His defenses would crumble at the slightest excuse to pick up a drink. What he had learned about alcoholism hadn't helped him at all.

In Fred's words, "I saw that willpower and self-knowledge wouldn't protect me against those strange mental blank spots. I'd never been able to understand people who said that a problem had them hopelessly defeated. I knew then. It was a crushing blow."

When two AA members came to visit him, they asked whether he was really beaten this time.

He confessed that he was. They snuffed out his last flicker of hope that he could do the job himself.

Fred listened to their description of AA's spiritual path and program of action. He found that their ideas weren't hard to swallow, although he found the action program pretty drastic. He'd have to throw out life-long beliefs. It wasn't easy, but once he took the steps suggested to him, he had the feeling that his alcoholism was under control, as indeed it was.

Fred discovered that spiritual principles could solve his problems. After that, his life became far more satisfying and useful than it ever was before. He said, "My old manner of life was by no means a bad one, but I wouldn't exchange the best moments of those days for the worst I have now."

Fred felt only the first nip of the wringer. Most alcoholics have to be mangled badly before they tackle their addiction.

Many doctors agree with the AA program. One doctor said that the stories of some alcoholics convinced him that they were 100 percent hopeless apart from divine help. He wouldn't have taken them at his hospital if he could have helped it. It was too heartbreaking. Although not religious, he expressed respect for the spiritual approach of the AA program. For most alcoholics, he said, there is no other solution.

Alcoholics at certain times have no defense against the first drink. Rarely can they or others provide such a defense. It must come from a Higher Power.

Chapter 4

We Agnostics

WE HOPE THAT THE FIRST chapters of this book have made clear the differences between alcoholic and nonalcoholic drinkers. If you can't quit even though you honestly want to or can't stop after the first drink, you're probably an alcoholic.

In most people, alcoholism is a disease that can be cured only by spiritual means. To people who consider themselves atheists or agnostics, this may seem impossible. But to continue drinking means disaster.

While the choice isn't always easy, it may not be as hard as you think. Many early AA members tried to avoid the issue, hoping they weren't true alcoholics. But soon they had to face the need for a spiritual foundation for their lives, or they would drink again.

If strong moral beliefs were all we needed, many of us could have quit drinking without AA.

But we couldn't. All our human resources failed us. Lack of power was our biggest problem. We had to find a power that was greater than ourselves.

This book was written to help alcoholics recover from their disease. Readers who consider themselves atheists or agnostics may have concerns about our references to "God" in the text. We've seen the faces of many newcomers light up as we explained our fellowship, and then fall at the mention of spirituality. They'd hoped to avoid the subject.

Many of us had these doubts. We considered belief in a Higher Power a weakness forced on us in childhood. We later rejected faith as weak or cowardly. How could the wars and violence throughout history be justified in the name of religion? At other times, we looked with awe at the night sky and wondered, "Who or what made all this?"

Let us reassure you. As soon as we opened ourselves to the idea of a Power greater than ourselves, we started getting results, even though we couldn't describe what we'd found. Our own concept of a Higher Power was enough to start with. When we accepted the possible existence of a Spirit of the Universe, we began to gain new energy and direction, provided we took some simple steps. A Higher Power is not overly demanding of those who seek a spiritual source of strength.

When God or a Higher Power is mentioned in this book, it refers to your own idea of the forces ruling the universe. Don't let prejudice against spirituality keep you from honestly asking yourself what it means to you. You're on your way when you can answer yes to the simple question, "Do I now believe, or am I willing to consider that there is some Power greater than myself?"

When people talked to us about spirituality, we thought, "If I could believe what they do, I'm sure it would work. But I can't." Most of us were encouraged when told that we could start at a basic level.

Because it's hard for us to accept things on faith, any mention of spirituality was likely to make us touchy. It wasn't easy to change this attitude, but we became more open-minded when we thought about how we were destroying our lives with alcohol. Liquor was the great persuader, even though it sometimes took a while.

Most people accept theories if they're based on fact. We believe theories about electricity, for example, because we want an explanation for what we see, feel, and use. Yet there is no perfect visual proof to back up many theories. Science has shown us, in fact, that outward appearances are often deceiving.

Consider the steel girder. According to scientists, it's a mass of spinning electrons governed by precise laws of physics. We believe them. But when someone suggests that there's a Creative Force at work, we try to convince ourselves it isn't so. We read philosophy books and get into lengthy arguments. We say this universe needs no Higher Power to explain it.

Does this mean that life came from nothing, means nothing, and is going nowhere? Instead of seeing ourselves as creations of a Higher Power, we insist that our human intelligence is the last word in all things.

If you are an agnostic or atheist, we ask you to set aside any prejudices you may have against organized religion. Whatever their faults, religious faiths have given purpose and direction to the lives of millions.

Before getting sober, we often amused ourselves by criticizing the spiritual beliefs of others. We should have noted that religion has helped people around the world enjoy stable, happy lives of service to others.

We chose to miss the beauty of the forest by focusing on the ugliness of some of its trees. We looked at the failings of some religious people and on this basis condemned them all. We accused them of intolerance, when we ourselves were intolerant. We never gave the spiritual side of life a chance.

In our personal stories, you'll find many ways in which alcoholics think of their Higher Power. Whether you agree with them or not doesn't matter. Each of us must decide who or what our Higher Power is. The fact is, it has worked miracles in our lives—miracles that would have been humanly impossible.

People of all backgrounds, including highly educated, sophisticated men and women, have come to accept a Higher Power and have seen their lives change dramatically. Despair and failure have been replaced by peace and a sense of direction. These people have discovered why they once ran into trouble at every turn. Countless alcoholics say that belief in a Higher Power is the most important factor in their recovery.

The world has seen more material progress in the last century than in the thousands of years before. Yet, the brains of humans in early civilizations were equal to those of people today according to experts in ancient history. In previous centuries, people were limited by superstition and tradition.

At the time of Columbus, the idea of a round earth was considered ridiculous. And the scientist

Galileo was almost put to death for claiming that the earth revolved around the sun and not vice versa.

A century ago, newspapers were afraid to report the Wright Brothers' 1903 airplane flight in Kitty Hawk, North Carolina. Hadn't scientists proven that humans could never fly? Hadn't God said flight was given only to birds? Just thirty years later, airplane travel was common.

Why shouldn't we be able to change our spiritual views, too? While drinking, we were miserable, we couldn't keep a job, and our relationships went to pieces. We felt useless and full of fear.

Wasn't a solution to our problems more important than scientific proof? When we saw others quit drinking by relying on a Higher Power, we stopped doubting its existence. Our ideas did not work and the idea of a Higher Power did. As we witnessed the effects of a Higher Power on recovering alcoholics, we began to feel like people who'd insisted that the Wright brothers would never fly.

A great attribute of the human species is its ability to reason, examine evidence, and draw conclusions. As atheists or agnostics, we weren't satisfied with ideas that wouldn't bear close inspection.

When we became alcoholics, crushed by the life we'd created from drinking, we had to decide whether we could accept the idea of a Higher Power. Using our reasoning ability as a bridge, we found we could walk toward the shore of spiritual belief. This gave us courage. The friendly hands of AA members reached out in welcome. But while many of us were grateful that we'd come this far, we leaned on our intellect for that last mile and didn't want to let go.

That was natural. But confidence in our intellect was a kind of faith, wasn't it? Hadn't we worshipped certain people, beliefs, material things, and even ourselves in the past? With higher motives, hadn't we worshipped the beauty of the sunset, the sea, or a flower? Hadn't each of us loved something or someone?

Since little of this came from pure reason, we couldn't say that we had no capacity for faith, love, or worship. In one way or another, we'd been living by faith all along.

Life wouldn't be worth much based on pure reason. It's hard to believe that life is nothing more than a mass of electrons coming from nothing, meaning nothing, and going nowhere. The electrons themselves seem more intelligent than that.

When people said that God made all things possible, we smiled in a superior way. We knew they were wrong. Actually, the need for a Higher

Power lies deep in the hearts of all humans. It may be hidden by personal troubles, self-importance, or worship of material things, but it's there in some form.

Faith in a Higher Power, no matter what its name, is a fact as old as humanity. It's as much a part of us as the feeling we have for a friend, although many of us had to lay our fears aside to find it. We discovered it deep within us, the only place it truly exists.

This book gives you a start. If it removes your prejudice, helps you to think honestly and search within yourself, then you can join us on the road to recovery. If you approach spiritual issues with an open mind, a personal belief is sure to come.

One AA member, a minister's son, considered himself an atheist. As a child, he rebelled at an overdose of religion and decided he didn't believe in God. For years, his life was filled with trouble and frustration. His business failed, and members of his family suffered insanity and fatal illness. He was bitter and depressed. As his alcoholism became worse, he was on the brink of mental and physical collapse.

One night in the hospital, he was visited by an AA member who'd had a spiritual experience. Our friend cried bitterly, "If there's a God, He certainly hasn't done anything for me!" But afterward he wondered, "Could it be that *all* the religious people I've known are wrong?" Then a thought flashed through his mind: "Who am I to say there is no God?"

The man got out of his hospital bed and on his knees, where he was overcome by the invisible presence of a Higher Power pouring over him like a flood. The walls he'd built over the years crumbled as he felt surrounded by the presence of Infinite Power and Love. He'd stepped from the bridge to the shore.

Our friend built his life on this cornerstone. Nothing has shaken it since. On that night, his alcoholic problem was taken away for good. When the thought of a drink returned, he found the idea revolting. His Higher Power had restored his sanity.

The miracle is plain. The man's dismal condition made him willing to believe. When he humbly offered himself to a Higher Power, he had a revelation. His spiritual awakening was sudden.

Some of us grow into it more slowly. But a Higher Power has been revealed to all of us who have sought it honestly. It has restored us to our right minds.

Chapter 5

How It Works

RARELY HAVE WE SEEN a person fail who has thoroughly followed our path. Those who don't recover are people who cannot or will not give themselves completely to this simple program. Usually they are unable to be honest with themselves. They aren't at fault. They seem to have been born that way. They cannot grasp a manner of living that demands rigorous honesty. Their chances are less than average. There are those, too, who suffer from mental disorders, but many do recover if they have the ability to be honest.

Our stories reveal what we used to be like, what happened, and what we are like now. If you want what we have and are willing to go to any length to get it, you're ready to take certain steps. Some of these we resisted, thinking we could find an easier way. But we could not.

We beg of you to be fearless and thorough from the start. Some of us have tried to hold on to our old ideas but got nowhere until we let go absolutely.

Remember that we deal with alcohol––cunning, baffling, powerful. Without help it is too much for us. But there is one who has all power. That one is God.

Half measures were useless. We stood at the turning point. We asked God's protection and care without reservation. Here are the steps we took, which are suggested as a program of recovery:

1. We admitted that we were powerless over alcohol and that our lives had become unmanageable.
2. We came to believe that a Power greater than ourselves could restore us to sanity.
3. We made a decision to turn our will and our lives over to the care of a Higher Power of our understanding.
4. We made a searching and fearless moral inventory of ourselves.
5. We admitted to our Higher Power, to ourselves, and to another human being the exact nature of our wrongs.
6. We were entirely ready to have our Higher Power remove all these defects of character.

7. We humbly asked our Higher Power to re-move our shortcomings.
8. We made a list of all persons we had harmed and became willing to make amends to them all.
9. We made direct amends to such people wherever possible, except when to do so would injure them or others.
10. We continued to take personal inventory and when we were wrong promptly admit-ted it.
11. We sought through prayer and meditation to improve our conscious contact with the Higher Power of our understanding, ask-ing only for guidance and the willingness to follow it.
12. Having had a spiritual awakening as the result of these steps, we tried to carry this message to alcoholics and to practice these principles in all our affairs.

Many of us exclaimed, "What an order! I can't go through with it." Don't worry. None of us has been able to follow this program perfectly. We are not saints. The point is that we are willing to grow along spiritual lines. The principles we have set down are guides to progress. We claim spiritual progress rather than spiritual perfection.

Our experience as alcoholics makes clear three pertinent ideas:

a. That we were alcoholic and could not manage our own lives.
b. That probably no human power could have relieved our alcoholism.
c. That a Higher Power could and would if sought.

We talk about turning our lives over to a Higher Power. What does this mean and why do we do it?

First, we must be convinced that running our lives on self-will isn't likely to work. We're almost always in conflict with someone, even when our motives are good. The alcoholic is like an actor who wants to run the show, constantly arranging the lights, scenery, and players. If only people would do as they were told, the show would be great. Everyone would be happy.

Actually, the actor trying to take charge may be a good person—kind, patient, generous, and even modest. On the other hand, the person may be mean, self-centered, and dishonest. But, like most people, he or she is usually somewhere in between.

When the show goes badly, the actor thinks life isn't fair and tries harder, demanding even more. Still, the play doesn't go smoothly. The actor admits to some of the blame but is sure that other people are more at fault. He or she is angry and full of self-pity.

These people have the false belief that they can get satisfaction from this world if only they manage it right. The manipulative actor makes others want to push back, producing confusion rather than harmony.

Such people are like retirees lying in the Florida sun complaining of the sad state of the nation or preachers who see nothing but sin all around. They're like criminals who claim society has done them wrong or alcoholics who have lost everything and are locked up. Weren't *most* of us concerned with ourselves first, our resentments, or our self-pity?

Selfishness and self-centeredness, we think, are the root of our troubles. Our fear, dishonesty, greed, and self-pity make us step on others' toes and they strike back. We later find that we've made selfish decisions that set us up to be hurt.

Our troubles, we think, are our own fault. Alcoholics are extreme examples of self-will run riot, although they usually don't think so. If we don't rid ourselves of this trait, it will kill us. But we can't do it without a Higher Power to direct us.

When we joined the AA program, we found a new spiritual direction and good things began to happen. We grew less interested in ourselves and more interested in others. As new power flowed into us, we enjoyed peace of mind. We were able to face life with confidence and began to lose our fear of the future. We were reborn.

We had to quit playing God because it didn't work. Our Higher Power had to take the director's role. Using this as our foundation, we were able to follow the AA path to freedom.

This brought us to Step Three. When we were sure we were ready, we prayed to our Higher Power, asking to be relieved of the bondage of self. We asked to have our burdens removed so we could help others. We asked to always do God's will.

It's best to take this step with a sponsor or other spiritual adviser. But you're better off meeting your Higher Power alone than confiding in a person who might not understand.

While praying, we used plain words and committed ourselves fully. When we were honest and humble, the effect was often sudden and powerful.

Next we began the fourth step. We did a personal housecleaning. This was new to some of us. But the benefits of our third step decision wouldn't last unless we faced the personality defects that got us into trouble in the first place. Drinking was just a symptom. We had to deal with causes.

A business that takes no inventory usually goes broke. The owner must learn the truth about the stock in trade. Damaged goods or those of no value are identified and discarded without regret. Business owners can't fool themselves about their inventories.

We did the same thing with our personal lives. We took stock honestly. First we looked for the flaws in our make-up that caused our failures. Being convinced that our inflated egos were at the root of our problems, we examined them closely.

Resentment destroys more alcoholics than anything else. It creates a spiritual block that goes beyond the mental and physical suffering caused by alcoholism. When the block is removed, the minds and bodies of alcoholics recover, too.

We wrote down our resentments, listing people, institutions, or principles that made us angry. Then we asked ourselves what the cause of our anger was. Usually, our self-esteem, ambitions, personal relationships, or bank accounts were threatened.

We reviewed our lives carefully. If we were honest, we saw that we'd blamed others for our troubles. The more we struggled and tried to get our own way, the worse things got. When we achieved a victory, it was short-lived. Plainly, a life of resentment is unhappy, allowing us to waste hours that could be useful.

Negative feelings shut us off from the sunlight of the Spirit. Resentments block spiritual growth and put us in dangerous territory. When alcoholic insanity returns, we drink again, and to drink is to die. Normal people can get away with anger, but for us it's poison.

Resentment List		
I resent	Cause of resentment	This affects my
Mr. Brown	Flirted with my wife, told her about my affair. May get my job at the office.	Sex relations, self-esteem (fear)
Mrs. Jones	She's weird, snubbed me. Put her husband in the hospital for drinking. He's my friend. She's a gossip.	Security, self-esteem (fear))
My employer	Unreasonable, unjust, overbearing. Threatens to fire me for drinking and padding expense account.	Personal relationship, self-esteem (fear)
My wife	Misunderstands me, nags. Attracted to Brown. Wants our house put in her name.	Pride, personal relationship, sex relations, security (fear)

Our resentment list showed that we'd given too much power to others and their imagined or real wrongs. We had to master our resentments, but how? We couldn't wish them away, any more than we could wish alcohol away.

Our attitude was the key. We had given others the power to control us. Our resentments would destroy our lives if we let them. We had to recognize that many other people are spiritually ill, too. For this reason we avoided arguing or striking back. We asked our Higher Power to help us show these people the same tolerance, pity, and patience that we would a sick friend.

We put aside the wrongs of others and looked at the error of our own ways. We didn't try to get back at people, and we refused to get involved in arguments. We wanted to make amends, not get angry. Our fourth step inventory was about *us*, not others. As we identified our faults, we listed them. Then we became willing to set the past straight.

The word "fear" appears many times in most resentment lists. Woven through the fabric of our lives, this evil thread set events into motion that touched almost everything we did. We had troubles we felt we didn't deserve, but usually we were the ones who started the ball rolling.

We also wrote down fears that had nothing to do with resentments. What caused them? Had our self-reliance failed us? Self-reliance was good as far as it went, but it could go only so far. When it filled us with pride, things tended to go wrong.

Trusting in a Power beyond ourselves is much more effective, we've found. We're in the world to play a useful role according to the gifts given to us. When we live by spiritual principles and rely upon a Higher Power to guide us, we can meet personal problems with serenity.

We don't apologize for our spiritual approach to life. The way we live demonstrates that faith in a Higher Power brings results. Throughout the ages, people have proved that faith is the way of strength, not weakness. When we pray to have our fears removed and to develop spiritually, we outgrow fear.

Our sexual behavior deserves attention, too. Opinions on the subject tend to run to extremes. One side says that sex is the lust of our lower natures and should be used only to create children. The other side says that if people had a lot more sex, the world's problems would go away.

We don't want to dictate the sexual behavior of others. Having sexual difficulties in a relationship is part of being human. But what can we do about them?

We review our past to find out where we've been selfish, dishonest, or inconsiderate. Whom had we hurt? Did we make others jealous, suspicious, or bitter? What did we do wrong, and what should we have done instead? We write it all down.

This helps us aim for healthy sexual relationships in the future. We ask our Higher Power for a new set of ideals and the ability to live up to them. After all, our sexuality is God-given and therefore good. We shouldn't use it lightly or selfishly, nor should we despise it.

We must be willing to grow toward our ideal by making amends to people we've hurt, provided that we don't injure them by doing so. In other words, we treat sex like any other problem. In meditation, we ask our Higher Power what to do in each situation and we wait for the answer.

Getting advice from others often helps, but we avoid talking to people who have extreme views about sex. Our Higher Power must be the final judge.

Suppose we stumble? Do we have to drink over it? If we're sorry for what we've done and want to mend our ways, we can move on without using alcohol. We'll have learned a lesson. If we continue to harm ourselves and others, we're quite sure to drink. These are the facts of our experience.

To sum up about our sexual conduct—we ask for guidance in each situation and the strength to do the right thing. If a relationship troubles us, we focus on helping others to quiet the powerful urges that would lead us back to old behaviors, and it prevents heartache.

If our inventory has been complete, we've written a lot. We've listed and analyzed our resentments. We've begun to understand how useless and harmful they are. We've started to learn patience and good will toward others, even our enemies. We've listed the people we've hurt by our behavior. We've become willing to straighten out the past as best we can.

In this book, you'll read over and over that faith did for us what we couldn't do for ourselves. We hope you're convinced that faith can remove whatever has blocked you from living on a spiritual plane. If you've already taken a personal inventory, you've made a good start. You've swallowed and digested some big chunks of truth about yourself.

Chapter 6

—

Into Action

AFTER REVIEWING OUR INVENTORY AND finding the weak spots in our character, we must take action to get rid of them. But first, we must admit to ourselves, our Higher Power, and another person the nature of these defects.

We may think we've done well just admitting them to ourselves, but this is seldom enough. We have to go farther. This brings us to the fifth step of the AA program—discussing our faults with another person, however hard it may seem.

Many alcoholics would be more inclined to take this step if given a good reason. The best is that keeping secrets may prevent us from recovering. Newcomers who keep secrets usually get drunk. They may have worked hard at the rest of the program, but they slip because they never finished their personal housecleaning.

Some alcoholics keep some of the worst items in their inventory. They only *think* they've lost their self-centeredness and fear, when they haven't really learned enough about humility, courage, and honesty to stay sober. They need to tell someone their entire life story.

Alcoholics lead double lives. Like actors, they show the sides of themselves they want others to see. They'd like to enjoy a good reputation but know they don't deserve it.

They worsen matters by drinking. Afterward, they're disgusted by their behavior. They worry about who saw them. But they quickly push their shameful thoughts down where no one can see them. Their anxiety never goes away, which makes them want to drink more.

Alcoholics spend thousands of dollars on doctors, but they seldom admit the truth about their drinking or follow medical advice. No wonder many health professionals have such a low opinion of alcoholics.

We must be totally honest with at least one trusted person if we're to live happily in this world. It's important that we tell our story to someone who'll understand but whose life won't be affected. Of course, we must select the person with great care.

Most alcoholics choose an AA sponsor who can keep confidences. Some talk to a professional with counseling skills. Our choice should be made carefully, though, because not all people with good credentials have the skills needed to help alcoholics recover.

Alcoholics who can't find a suitable person may postpone this step, but only if they resolve to take it at the first chance they get. The fifth step should not be put off any longer than necessary.

When we find the right person, we arrange a meeting and take our written inventory, ready for a long talk. We explain what we're doing and why it's crucial. The person may be honored by our trust.

Pocketing our pride, we shine a light on all the dark corners of our past. The rule is that we must be tough about our own failings but tolerant of other people's. If we've held back nothing, we're usually at peace and can look the world in the eye. Our fears fall away as we start to feel the presence of a Higher Power.

While we may have had spiritual beliefs before, we now begin to have spiritual experiences. The feeling that our drinking problem has disappeared may come over us. We sense that we're walking hand in hand with a Higher Power.

Returning home, we sit quietly and review our fifth step. We thank our Higher Power for the chance to share our history with a trusted person. Opening this book, we read the Twelve Steps again to see if we've left anything out. Have we built a strong foundation? Can we walk toward the future as free beings?

If we're satisfied with our fifth step, we move on to Step Six. Here, we ask our Higher Power for the willingness to have our character defects removed. We may start with a prayer, such as, "My Creator, I am now willing for you to have all of me, good and bad. I pray that you remove the defects of character that stand in the way of my usefulness in this world. Grant me strength to go out from here and follow your will." We have then taken Step Seven.

Steps Eight and Nine are next, requiring more action. Referring to our inventory, we list all the persons we've harmed. After serious self-searching, we prepare to make amends—to sweep away the wreckage of the past resulting from our self-centeredness. If we're not quite ready, we ask for help to gain the willingness we need. Remember, we agreed to go to any lengths for victory over alcohol.

If you feel awkward about approaching some of the people on your list, let us reassure you. You need not tell everyone about the spiritual aspect of your amends. It might put them off.

Although we're trying to set our lives in order, our main goal is to serve our Higher Power and the people around us. It's not wise to announce that we've got religion to those still suffering from the pain we caused them. Getting branded as religious fanatics might spoil our credibility. But the people we approach will surely be impressed by our desire to correct past mistakes.

People are more interested in the actions we take than in spiritual talk. However, if mention of our Higher Power serves a good purpose, we speak of our convictions with tact and common sense.

How should we talk with people we used to hate? They may have hurt us more than we hurt them. Although our resentments may have faded, we're still not overjoyed about admitting our faults to them.

Still, we must grit our teeth and do the right thing. It's harder to apologize to an enemy than to a friend, but it does us more good. So with a sincere and forgiving spirit, we confess our former errors and express our regret.

Under no condition should we find fault or argue with others. We simply say that we are trying to make amends for our past behavior in order to recover from our drinking problem. If we don't sweep off *our* side of the street, we'll make no progress. When we're calm, honest, and open about this, we'll be pleased with the results.

Sometimes others apologize for their part, melting away old feuds in an hour. Our former enemies may praise what we're doing and wish us well. It shouldn't matter, though, if they brush us off and walk away. We've made our amends in good faith and have done our part. It's water over the dam.

Most alcoholics owe money. As recovering alcoholics, we don't dodge creditors. We tell them we had a drinking problem—something they probably already knew. We don't hide our alcoholism because of fears we have about the possible financial fall-out.

Approached in this way, even hard-hearted creditors can surprise us. We admit that our drinking made us slow to pay our bills in the past. We're sorry and will do our best to re-pay the money we owe. We must lose our fear of creditors no matter what. Otherwise, we're likely to drink.

Some of us could lose our jobs or be sent to jail if people knew the things we've done. We may have padded expense accounts or failed to make alimony or child support payments. An ex-spouse may have a warrant out for our arrest. Problems with authorities are common among alcoholics.

Guidelines for making amends include a willingness to go to any lengths to set things right. We ask for the strength to do the honorable thing even if we might get fired or sent to jail. We must not hold back.

Because those close to us may be affected by our actions, we shouldn't be hasty or foolish, however. We might cause trouble for innocent people. Before we take action, we get their consent. Then, with the help of our Higher Power, we do what needs to be done.

A man we know who remarried during recovery hadn't made support payments to his first wife, with whom he lived during his drinking days. She was furious, went to court, and got an order for his arrest. In recovery, he was just getting his head above water financially.

He could have been a hero and said to the judge, "Here I am, take me away." But this wouldn't help either family. We suggested that he write to his first wife, admitting his faults and asking forgiveness. He wrote her a letter, enclosed some money, and outlined his intentions to make future payments. He said he was willing to go to jail if she insisted. Of course, she didn't, and the whole problem has long since been solved.

A friend, while drinking, took money from a business rival, giving him no receipt. Later he denied having taken the money and made the rival look bad publicly, damaging his reputation.

In recovery, our friend felt he'd done harm that could never be undone. If he tried, he feared it would hurt his current business partner's reputation, disgrace his own family, and destroy his career. What right did he have to do this to people who depended on him?

After talking with his wife and current business partner, he decided it was better to risk the consequences than to continue being guilty of such slander. He placed the outcome in the hands of his Higher Power. He knew that if he didn't, he'd probably drink again and lose everything anyhow.

He attended church for the first time in years and made his confession there. People responded warmly and he regained their respect and trust.

Most alcoholics have gotten tangled in romantic relationships outside the home. In this respect, they aren't much worse than other people. But drinking does complicate matters. After years with an alcoholic, the person's mate gets worn out, resentful, and withdrawn. What else would you expect? Then the alcoholic begins to feel lonely and full of self-pity.

Some of us started hanging around clubs and bars looking for affairs. We hoped to find someone who would "understand" us. In fairness, the sexual partners we chose were often good people.

How should we handle these situations? Alcoholics in long-term relationships who get involved with a third party are often deeply sorry, especially if their partners at home have already gone through hell for them.

Should a partner who doesn't know about an affair be told? Not always, we think. If the person suspects the truth, should we confess in detail? Maybe not. But certainly we should admit that our behavior was wrong.

Some partners insist on knowing who the third party is. We probably have no right to reveal this. There's no point in naming a person who might become the target of our partner's jealousy. We apologize for our behavior and promise not to repeat it. We can't do more. While we don't wish to lay down rules, we've often found this to be the best approach.

No outsider can advise a couple about how to repair their relationship. Perhaps both partners will decide to let bygones be bygones. Each might pray about it, with the other's happiness in mind. Because jealousy is a powerful human emotion, an approach by its flank is often better than head-on combat.

Even if our families hadn't been disrupted by our love affairs, other matters need our attention. Some alcoholics think that all they need to do is quit drinking. True, they must give up alcohol. But the person who's stopped drinking is a long way from making amends to a family harmed over a long period of time. Most families have shown amazing patience with the alcoholic. If this weren't so, many of us would have no homes today. We might be dead.

Alcoholics are like tornadoes roaring through the lives of others. They've broken hearts and destroyed relationships. Their self-centered habits have kept their homes in turmoil. Ex-drinkers who say that it's enough to give up alcohol remind us of the farmer who climbed out of his cyclone cellar to find his home destroyed. He turned to his wife, saying "Don't see anything wrong here, Ma—ain't it great the wind stopped blowin'?"

Newly sober alcoholics face a long period of rebuilding. Saying they're sorry isn't enough. They must sit down with their families and review the past as they see it, not criticizing anyone in the process.

Family members have their faults, too. But as alcoholics, we multiplied their problems. So we clean house, asking our Higher Power each morning to show us how to be patient, tolerant, kind, and loving.

The spiritual life is not just an idea in our heads. We must live it. Families who aren't interested in our spiritual program shouldn't be pushed. Their attitudes will change over time. Our behavior will convince them more than our words. We must remember that years of living with a drunk would make anyone cautious.

The damage we've caused may never be fully repaired, but this shouldn't worry us if we can honestly say that we'd make good if we could.

When we can't arrange a personal meeting with someone we've harmed, we write an honest letter. A meeting may be postponed if there's a good reason, but as a general rule delays should be avoided.

When dealing with people we've harmed, we should be sensible, tactful, considerate, and humble, but we don't need to crawl. As the creations of our Higher Power, we always stand in dignity.

If we're painstaking about this phase of our development, we'll be amazed before we're half-way through. We're going to know a new freedom and a new happiness. We won't regret the past nor wish to shut the door on it. We'll comprehend the word serenity and we'll know peace.

No matter how far down the scale we've gone, we'll see how our experience can benefit others. That feeling of uselessness and self-pity will disappear. We'll lose interest in selfish things and gain interest in our fellows. Self-seeking will slip away. Our whole attitude and outlook upon life will change.

Fear of people and of economic insecurity will leave us. We'll intuitively know how to handle situations that used to baffle us. We'll suddenly realize that our Higher Power is doing for us what we could not do for ourselves. Are these extravagant promises? We think not. They're being fulfilled among us—sometimes quickly, sometimes slowly. They will always materialize if we work for them.

This brings us to Step Ten, which tells us to continue our personal inventory on a daily basis, correcting mistakes as we go along. In the AA program of recovery, we have a new spiritual approach to life that helps us grow in understanding and effectiveness. This continues for a lifetime.

We must guard against the tendency to be selfish, dishonest, resentful, or fearful. When any of these feelings arise, we ask our Higher Power to remove them. We find someone we trust and share the problem right away. If we've harmed anyone, we make amends without delay. After this, we turn our thoughts to someone we can help. Love and tolerance is our code.

We've ceased fighting anyone or anything, even alcohol. The return of our sanity almost always removes our desire to drink. But if tempted, we pull back as if from a hot flame.

The miracle is that our ability to react sanely seems to have come about naturally. We're neither fighting temptation nor avoiding it. We feel as though we've been placed in a neutral position—safe and protected.

We haven't sworn off liquor. Instead, the problem has been lifted. We're neither cocky nor afraid as long as we keep in fit spiritual condition.

While it's easy to rest on our laurels, we're headed for trouble if we do. Alcoholism is sneaky. We're not cured. What we have is a daily reprieve that depends upon maintaining a healthy spiritual condition.

We must follow the guidance of our Higher Power in all our activities. We strive to serve the God of our understanding rather than ourselves. Exercising our willpower in this way is a proper use of the will.

If we've taken the suggestions in this book about relying on a Higher Power, we've begun to sense a flow of spiritual energy within us. But we must do more, and that means more action.

Step Eleven suggests prayer and meditation as a regular practice. When you go to bed, review your day. Were you resentful, selfish, dishonest, or afraid? Do you owe someone an apology? Have you kept something to yourself that should be discussed with another person? Were you kind and loving toward all? What could you have done better?

As you do this step, avoid drifting into worry or remorse, for that lessens your usefulness to others. After reviewing your day, pray to be forgiven for your mistakes and ask for guidance in correcting them.

When arising in the morning, go over your day's plans, asking your Higher Power to direct you. Pray to be free of self-pity, dishonesty, or self-seeking motives. Then you can confidently approach the hours ahead on a higher spiritual plane, not acting on impure motives.

If you're unsure of how to proceed, ask for inspiration, guidance, and direction. Then relax. You may be surprised at how the right answers come naturally after you've tried this method for a while.

What used to seem like occasional inspirations will become a regular part of your thinking. Newly sober alcoholics still lack experience, of course, and shouldn't be expected to be inspired at all times. Occasional overconfidence might result in some wrong actions and ideas. Still, as time passes, your intuition will become more and more reliable.

As recovering alcoholics, we usually end our meditation by asking for whatever we need to solve our problems. We pray to be free of self-will. We avoid selfish requests, although we may ask for help if it will benefit others. We've learned that praying just for ourselves wastes time and doesn't work.

When practical, we invite families or friends to join us in meditation. If we follow a tradition of morning devotions, we continue it. We may memorize a few prayers that focus on the principles we've been discussing. Good inspirational books are available, as well. Sometimes people with spiritual beliefs have helpful insights.

During the day, we pause when we're anxious or doubtful and ask for direction. We remind ourselves that we're not running the show and pray for the willingness to follow our Higher Power's guidance.

When we do this, we're in less danger of getting agitated, fearful, angry, or sorry for ourselves. It makes us more effective and helps us avoid foolish mistakes. We don't tire as easily as we once did, because we no longer burn energy foolishly, trying to arrange life to suit ourselves.

Alcoholics have little self-discipline. So we must get it from a Higher Power. Above all, we need action and more action. "Faith without works is dead."

This brings us to Step Twelve, which is described in the next chapter.

Chapter 7

―――

Working with Others

NOTHING PROTECTS US AGAINST RELAPSE more than helping another alcoholic. When all else fails, Step Twelve works. Carry the message to other alcoholics!

You can help the suffering alcoholic in a way no one else can. You can get the person's confidence when others fail. Remember that he or she is very ill.

Twelfth step work gives our lives new meaning. We've had the experience of helping others recover and seeing their loneliness disappear. We've become part of a network of friends and watched the AA fellowship grow around us. Frequent contact with other alcoholics is the bright spot in our lives.

If you don't know any problem drinkers who want to get sober, you can find some by asking health professionals or the staff of treatment centers. They'll be glad to direct you.

Don't start as a preacher or reformer. You won't help people if you make them defensive. So cooperate, never criticize. Being helpful is our only aim.

Find out all you can about the practicing alcoholics you meet. If they don't want to stop drinking, don't waste your time coaxing them. You may spoil a later chance. This is good advice for the families of alcoholics, too. It's important for them to be patient.

It often helps to talk with the drinker's partner or family for background details. You can find out how severe the alcoholic's problem is. With this knowledge, you can put yourself in the drinker's place and imagine how you'd like to be treated if the tables were turned.

Sometimes, twelfth step work is best put off until the drinker has gone on a binge. The family may disagree with this, but unless the alcoholic is in grave physical condition, it's worth the risk.

Don't try to deal with alcoholics who are in the middle of a binge unless their behavior is so out of control that the family needs your help. Wait until the spree is over, or at least until the drinker is making some sense. Then suggest that a family member or friend ask the alcoholic whether he or she wants to quit for good.

If the answer is yes, the person should be introduced to you as someone who has stayed sober in AA and tries to help others who have a drinking problem. The drinker should know that it's part of your recovery program, and you'll be glad to talk to him or her.

Never force yourself on the alcoholic who doesn't want to see you. Advise the family not to talk much about you in advance or beg the drinker to meet you.

There are no specific rules for twelfth step work, but this book should be offered to the alcoholic. Although the family needs to follow their own judgment, urge them not to rush things, for it might spoil their chances to help.

Actually, twelfth step work is more effective when the alcoholic is not contacted through the family, but rather by a health professional or other outsider. Alcoholics who need to go to a hospital or treatment center should be offered the chance for inpatient care, but they shouldn't be forced unless they're violent. Let a health professional guide the alcoholic in this regard.

As alcoholics get better in a hospital or treatment facility, they may be put in touch with AA members who do twelfth step work. Families should be left out of these first contacts. Alcoholics need to see that no one will pressure them or their families about joining AA. It's best for these first meetings to occur while the alcoholic is still jittery or depressed and therefore more open to the AA message.

Your meetings should be private. You can start the conversation in a light, general way. Then turn the topic to some aspect of drinking. Talk a little about your old drinking habits, symptoms, and experiences and encourage the alcoholic to do the same.

If you let the alcoholic talk freely when you meet, it will help you decide how to proceed. Of course, some alcoholics have little to say. In such cases, briefly describe your drinking career. But for now, don't describe exactly how you managed to quit. If the person is in a serious mood, relate some of the troubles liquor caused you, being careful not to preach. If the person's mood is light, tell funny stories about your drinking days and encourage him or her to do the same.

When the alcoholic sees that you know the drinking game, it's time to describe yourself as an alcoholic. Talk about how confused and stuck you were, how you finally understood that you were sick, and your struggle to stop drinking. Describe the twisted thinking that afflicts alcoholics, tempting them to take the first drink, which only leads to a spree. Real alcoholics will understand you at once. They may match your stories with some of their own.

When you're convinced that you're dealing with an alcoholic, explain the hopeless nature of the disease. Describe from your own experience how the willpower of an alcoholic is paralyzed after the first drink.

At this stage, don't mention this book unless the alcoholic has already seen it and wants to discuss it. Don't label the person an alcoholic. Problem drinkers need to draw their own conclusions. Those who insist that they can still control their liquor intake should be told it may be possible—if their alcoholism isn't too far gone. But insist that drinkers who have the full-blown disease have little chance to recover on their own.

Refer to alcoholism as an illness, a fatal disease. Talk about the conditions of the body and mind that go with it. Include details from your personal experience. Explain that many alcoholics never realize the danger they're in. Most doctors won't tell them the truth about the disease unless it serves some practical purpose. You are different. You offer a solution.

At this point, many alcoholics are ready to admit that they have the symptoms of alcoholism.

If the alcoholic's doctor is willing to confirm the diagnosis, so much the better. Even those who aren't ready to accept their condition are likely to be curious about how you got well. If so, tell them exactly what happened to you.

Stress the spiritual approach of the AA program. Alcoholics who don't believe in God—or don't know what they believe in—should be told that they don't have to agree with anyone else's concept of God. They can choose whatever spiritual belief makes sense to them. The main thing is that they become willing to trust in a Power greater than themselves and that they live by spiritual principles.

In twelfth step work, it's best to use everyday language and avoid religious terms. There's no point in raising people's resistance to the program. Don't make a confused person more confused. Don't get into religious issues, no matter what your personal convictions are.

Many alcoholics belong to churches. Their religious education may be better than yours, making them wonder how you can possibly add to what they already know. But they'll be curious to learn why their own beliefs haven't helped them and yours seem to.

Such people are examples of the failure of faith alone to cure alcoholism. To be effective, faith has to be backed up by unselfish action.

AA prospects shouldn't feel that you plan to teach them about spirituality. Freely admit that they may know more than you. Point out, though, that their faith alone wasn't enough to keep them from drinking. Your personal story may show such alcoholics where they failed to practice the principles that they know so well.

AA members should not speak for any one brand of spirituality when they do twelfth step work. We deal with the general principles found in most faiths.

Outline the AA program of action. Explain how you took an honest inventory of yourself and straightened out your past, and why working with other alcoholics helps you stay sober. It's important for people to understand that twelfth step work plays a vital part in your own recovery.

Make it clear that they owe you nothing. Your only hope is that when they get sober they'll offer the same help to other alcoholics. Suggest the importance of placing the welfare of others first.

Stress the fact that they're not under any pressure. They don't have to see you again if they don't want to. Don't be offended if they don't. They have probably helped you more than you have helped them.

If your talk has been quiet and sincere, you may have made a friend. If you've disturbed the person about his or her alcoholism, that's all to the good. The more hopeless the active alcoholic feels, the better. The person will be more likely to change.

Many practicing alcoholics give reasons why they don't need AA. Some resist doing a drastic housecleaning and sharing it with others. Don't argue. Explain how you once felt the same but think you wouldn't have made progress without taking action.

In your first conversation, describe the fellowship of Alcoholics Anonymous. If the person shows interest, give him or her your copy of this book.

Unless the alcoholic wants to carry the discussion further, don't wear out your welcome. Allow the person time to think over what you've said. If you continue the conversation, let the alcoholic steer the topic in any direction he or she chooses.

Some alcoholics are anxious to proceed at once, and you may be tempted to go along with them. This can be a mistake. Those who later have problems are likely to say you rushed them. You'll be most successful if you don't show a passion for crusading.

Never talk down to an alcoholic from a moral or spiritual hilltop. Simply lay out AA's kit of spiritual tools for the person to think about. Offer your friendship and fellowship. Tell the alcoholic who has a desire to get well that you'll do anything to help.

You may have to let go of alcoholics who aren't really looking for a solution. This also applies to drinkers who expect financial help or hope to be nursed after a binge. Wait until they have a change of heart. This may happen when they've been hurt some more.

Alcoholics who show a sincere interest in the AA program and want to see you again should be offered this book. After they've looked at it, they can decide whether they want to proceed. However, no one should pressure them, including you, their family, or their friends. If they're going to find a spiritual program, the desire must come from within.

Alcoholics who think they can control their drinking using some method other than the AA program should be encouraged to follow their conscience. In AA we have no monopoly on spirituality. We just have a program that worked for us. But point out that alcoholics have a lot in common and that you'd like to stay friends, no matter what the person's decision. Let it go at that.

Don't feel let down if the person doesn't respond right away. Find another alcoholic to help. You're sure to find someone eager for what you have to offer. It's a waste of time to chase alcoholics who can't or won't be helped. When such people are left alone, they often realize that they can't do it on their own.

If you spend too much time on any one individual, you pass up chances to help others who are ready to try the program. A friend told us he failed entirely with his first six prospects. Now he realizes if he'd stuck with them, he might have deprived many others of a chance to recover.

If you're meeting someone for the second time who's read this book and is prepared to follow AA's recovery program, you can offer much practical advice. Let the person know that you're available to hear his or her story, but don't insist on it if the person prefers to work with someone else.

Some alcoholics are broke and homeless. AA members often help these people find jobs or even offer a little financial aid. But it's important not to go too far. A few AA members take alcoholics into their homes for short periods. Do this only with great care. Be sure it's all right with your family.

Make certain that an alcoholic isn't taking advantage of you. If you let yourself be exploited, you'll only cause harm. Letting an alcoholic get by with such behavior aids in the person's destruction, not his or her recovery.

While you should never avoid twelfth step work, always be sure you're doing the right thing when you reach out to another alcoholic. Helping others is the cornerstone of your recovery. A kindness here and there isn't enough. You must be available every day of your life.

Some nights you'll go without sleep. You may have to give up some leisure time or take some hours off work. You'll find yourself counseling the families of alcoholics and driving to treatment centers, courts, and jails. Your telephone may ring at all hours. Your family may feel neglected at times. You may have to get someone to help you if an alcoholic becomes dangerous or violent.

Taking alcoholics into our homes for more than a short time is not a good idea. It's bad for the alcoholic and sometimes brings serious distress to our families.

If an alcoholic doesn't respond to your help, you can still reach out to his or her family while continuing to be friendly with the alcoholic. The family should be offered your way of life. If they practice the spiritual principles of the AA program, there's a much better chance that the drinker in the family will recover. Even if the alcoholic doesn't stay sober, the program will make the family's life easier.

Most alcoholics with an honest desire to recover don't want or need much material help. Those who cry for money and shelter before getting sober are on the wrong track. Yet we do share our resources when it's warranted. This may seem contradictory, but we don't think so.

It's not the matter of giving that's in question, but when and how to give. That can make the difference between failure and success. When we go too far, the alcoholic starts relying upon us rather than upon a Higher Power.

Some alcoholics claim they can't master alcohol until their material needs are met. This is nonsense. Some of us have learned this truth the hard way. Anyone who depends upon other people before relying on a Higher Power will not stop drinking.

Emphasize the idea that alcoholics can get well without leaning on others. The only requirement is that they trust in a Higher Power and clean house.

Some alcoholics find themselves in the middle of a divorce, separated from their partners, or living in a strained family situation. They need to patch things up with their families as best they can and explain the new principles they're trying to live by. Then they must put these principles into action at home—if they still have a home.

While the family may be somewhat at fault, that shouldn't concern the alcoholic. Recovering alcoholics should demonstrate their spiritual program by the way they live.

At home, the ex-drinker should avoid arguments and fault-finding like the plague. This may be hard to do in some families, but it's essential if progress is expected. After a few months, positive results will be evident. Family members who couldn't get along before will discover a common ground on which to meet. Little by little, the family may see their own defects and admit them. Eventually, problems can be discussed in a helpful and friendly manner.

After the family has seen the positive effects of AA's way of life, they may want to become involved, too. This should happen naturally over time—but only if the alcoholic stays sober and remains considerate and helpful no matter what others say or do. Of course, we all fall below this standard at times. But we must hasten to repair any damage we have caused if we hope to avoid drinking again.

The alcoholic who is divorced or separated should avoid rushing a reunion. The ex-drinker should focus on his or her recovery. The partner needs to understand the alcoholic's new way of life. If the two decide to become a couple again, it must be on a better basis, since their previous relationship didn't work. This means that both must adopt a new attitude and spirit.

Sometimes it's in everyone's best interests for a couple to remain apart. No rule can be laid down about this. Let the alcoholic practice his or her AA program on a daily basis. If the time for living together comes, it will be clear to both partners.

Don't let alcoholics claim that they can't recover unless they get their families back. This isn't so. Some partners will never come back. Remind the alcoholic that recovery doesn't depend upon other people. It depends upon a relationship with a Higher Power. We've seen alcoholics get well whose families never returned. We've seen others relapse when the family came back too soon.

Working with newly sober alcoholics means walking a spiritual path with them on a day-by-day basis. If you persist, amazing things will happen. Looking back, we realize that the results of turning our own lives over to a Higher Power were better than anything we could have planned. Following this path, newcomers to AA can soon live in a new and wonderful world, no matter what their lives were like before.

When working with alcoholics and their families, never take part in their quarrels. You may spoil your chance to help. Tell the family that alcoholics are sick people and should be treated accordingly. Warn them not to say or do things that might arouse resentment or jealousy. Point out that the alcoholic's character defects aren't going to vanish overnight. Show them that a period of growth is involved. When they lose patience, remind them that they're blessed by the fact that the alcoholic isn't drinking anymore.

If you have solved your own family problems, tell the newcomer's family how you did it. In this way, you'll help them get on track without being critical. The story of how you and your family recovered together is better than any type of criticism.

If we're spiritually fit, we can resist any temptation. People have said that alcoholics shouldn't go where liquor is served. They urge us to keep it out of our homes and stay away from friends who drink. They advise us to avoid movies with drinking scenes. They warn us to stay out of bars and to request that our friends hide their bottles when we visit. They think we mustn't be reminded of alcohol in any way.

These conditions aren't always necessary. First of all, we can't avoid all exposure to liquor. Anyone who can't face this still has an alcoholic mind. There's something wrong with the spiritual path of a person who can recover only in a remote place like the Greenland Ice Cap. Even there, a native might show up with a bottle of scotch and ruin everything. Ask any alcoholic who's gone far from home to escape this disease.

In our belief, any method of fighting alcoholism that removes all temptation is bound to fail. Alcoholics who try to hide from liquor may succeed for a while, but they usually wind up on a bigger binge than ever. We have tried these methods, and they've always failed.

Our rule is not to avoid places where people are drinking if we have a legitimate reason for being there. This includes clubs, dances, receptions, weddings, and even ordinary parties. To those who are close to alcoholics, this may seem like tempting fate, but that's rarely the case.

You'll note that we put an important condition on being around alcohol. Recovering alcoholics should have a legitimate reason for being where liquor is served. They should ask themselves, "Do I have a good social, business, or personal reason for going to this place? Or am I expecting second-hand pleasure from watching others drink?"

If you answer these questions honestly, you don't have to be afraid. Do whatever seems best. But be sure you're on solid spiritual ground before you decide. Make certain your motive is pure. Don't think of what you'll get from the occasion.

Think of what you can bring to it. If you feel shaky, you'd better work with another alcoholic instead.

There's no point in moping around where people are drinking, recalling the good old days. If you're there for a celebration, try to increase the pleasure of those around you. If it's a business event, attend to matters with a positive attitude. If you're with a friend who wants to eat in a bar, don't be afraid to go along. Let your friends know they don't have to change their habits on your account.

When the time is right, explain to friends why alcohol disagrees with you. If you make this clear, few people will urge you to drink. In the old days, you withdrew from life. Now you're getting back into the world. Don't start hiding again just because your friends drink.

Your job is to be where you can be of most service to others. Never hesitate to go where you can be useful, even if it's a bad neighborhood or other disagreeable place. If your motives are pure, your Higher Power will protect you.

Many of us keep liquor in our homes to serve to friends who aren't alcoholics. Not all AA members agree on this issue. Each family must decide how to handle this matter on their own.

We're careful never to criticize social drinkers. This attitude doesn't help anyone. Most newcomers expect us to disapprove of liquor, and they're relieved when we don't. A spirit of intolerance might put off people whose lives could otherwise be saved. A critical attitude won't change people's minds. No one wants to hear a lecture about alcohol by someone who hates it.

Some day we hope that Alcoholics Anonymous will increase the public's understanding of alcoholism. But people won't be enlightened if we have a bitter or hostile attitude. Drinkers won't stand for it. Our problems were our fault. Bottles were just a symptom. Besides, we've stopped fighting anybody or anything. We have to!

Chapter 8

———

To the Partners of Alcoholics

EVERY PERSON WITH A DRINKING problem affects the lives of others—often partners who fear the alcoholic's next drink. People close to the alcoholic are frustrated watching the person waste his or her life.

Alanon was created as a safe place for the partners, relatives, and friends of alcoholics. Alanon members offer support and love. They know, as few others do, what it's like to live with a problem drinker. They are proof that no difficulty is too great to overcome.

As the partners of alcoholics, we have had long experience with hurt pride, frustration, self-pity, misunderstanding, and fear. We've suffered daily. We've gone from being overly sympathetic to being bitter and resentful, always hoping that the alcoholic would return to normal one day.

In our loyalty, we were self-sacrificing. We told lies to protect our pride and our partners' reputations. We prayed, begged, and were patient. Some of us struck out viciously and then ran away. We were filled with fear. Some of us had love affairs as a way of getting back.

Our homes became battlegrounds. Then we kissed and made up. Friends told us to leave, and we did—only to return, hoping things would improve. When our alcoholic partners vowed to quit drinking, we believed them even though no one else did. In a few days, weeks, or months, they came home drunk again.

Friends didn't visit our homes because they never knew when it was safe. We rarely went out, as our partners usually sneaked so many drinks that they spoiled everyone's fun. When they made the supreme effort and drank nothing, their self-pity made others uncomfortable.

Few of us enjoyed financial security. Our alcoholic partners were either on the brink of being fired or had already lost their jobs. An armored car couldn't have brought their paycheck envelopes home unopened. Our joint checking accounts melted like snow in June.

Sometimes our partners had affairs that broke our hearts. How cruel to be told that a lover understood our partner better than we did!

We were followed by creditors. The police came to our doors. Our partners sometimes brought home shady friends and then criticized us for not welcoming them. The next day they'd act decent again, and we'd forgive and try to forget.

Those of us who had children tried to hold their love and cover up for our partners. We even became the sole support of the family, facing hardship when our partners no longer brought home a paycheck.

The drinking parent sometimes hit the children, kicked down doors, or smashed things. We told them that their alcoholic dad or mom was sick—something very close to the truth.

At this point, some of us left, but most stayed. If we got drunk ourselves for revenge, it backfired because our partners seemed to like it. We tried to pull ourselves together, then fell apart at each new setback.

Some of us consulted doctors about our partner's disease. We described the alcoholic's physical and mental symptoms, including the depression, remorse, and feelings of inferiority.

A few of us watched our partners enter the last stages of alcoholism. They were admitted to treatment centers or hospitals, or even put in jail. Some had hallucinations and became psychotic. Death was near for some.

Naturally, we made our own mistakes along the way. Many of them were due to our ignorance about the disease of alcoholism. We dimly sensed that we were dealing with sick people. If we'd fully understood the disease, we might have handled things better.

How could men and women who claimed to love their families be so cruel? Just when we convinced ourselves such people weren't capable of love, they surprised us with fresh promises and loving attention. They'd be their old sweet selves for a while, only to break the bonds between us once more.

When asked why they drank again, they gave some lame excuse or none at all. It was heartbreaking. Could we have made a big mistake in choosing our partner? When drunk, the person was a stranger who seemed as far away as though a great wall stood between us.

Even if these alcoholics didn't love their families, how could they be so blind about themselves? What happened to their judgment, common sense, and willpower? Couldn't they see that liquor was ruining them? Why did those who admitted that they had a problem go right back out and drink?

Perhaps your partner has been living in that alcoholic world. You can see that he or she really loves you. If you were once compatible, the chances are that you've been torn apart by the disease of alcoholism. Recovering alcoholics generally become good partners and parents when they adopt the AA program.

The nonalcoholic partner should avoid criticizing what the alcoholic says and does. Alcoholics should be treated as though they had pneumonia or some other serious disease, which they do.

Of course, some alcoholics are bad characters to begin with, and no amount of patience will change them. They are the first to use this book as a club over their partners. They mustn't get by with this. Partners are better off leaving them than allowing them to ruin the lives of their families. After all, the alcoholic *does* have a way to stop drinking if he or she really wants to.

Alcoholics generally fall into four categories.

Category 1: Those who drink regularly or drink heavily under certain conditions. These alcoholics may spend too much money on liquor. They may be slowing down mentally and physically and not realize it.

Sometimes they embarrass their family and friends. They insist that they can handle their liquor, and that their drinking is harmless or is an important part of doing business. They'd be insulted if called alcoholics.

Others decide to slow down their drinking or manage to stop completely. Those who can't stop have a good chance of becoming true alcoholics.

Category 2: Those who can't stop even when they want to or who lose control of their behavior once they start. These drinkers admit that they've gone too far, but promise to stop. They've tried ways of cutting down or quitting with or without help.

After each binge, they are full of remorse and say they want to give up alcohol for good. As soon as they feel better, they start planning how they can drink in moderation next time.

Alcoholics in this category sometimes drink in the morning or during the day to steady their nerves. They may be losing their friends or their jobs may suffer, but they haven't yet ruined their lives. They're starting to realize that they can't drink like other people.

These are the signs of real alcoholism. As we say in the fellowship, "They *want to* want to stop."

Category 3: Those who have passed through Category 2 and gone much further. Drinkers with more severe disease have usually lost their friends. Their home lives are a wreck, and they can't keep a job. They may have started entering clinics, treatment centers, and hospitals.

They admit they can't drink like other people but don't know why. They cling to the idea that they'll still find a way to stop. They may desperately want to, but can't. Actually, there's considerable hope for these alcoholics, as we'll soon show.

Category 4: Those who have been admitted to one institution after another. These drinkers are severely alcoholic and may become violent or psychotic when drunk. They may have hallucinations. Sometimes they drink the day they are discharged from treatment.

Doctors shake their heads over these patients, although the future may not be as dark as it seems. Many of these alcoholics still manage to recover.

Oddly enough, the drinkers in Category 1 can be the hardest to deal with. They enjoy alcohol. It makes them feel creative. Their friends have fun drinking with them when it doesn't go too far. We, too, have spent many happy evenings with them, talking and laughing. They're entertaining at parties.

The first rule in dealing with these alcoholics is to avoid getting angry. If your partner becomes so difficult that you decide to leave temporarily, don't leave in anger. Patience and friendliness are important.

Don't tell your partner how to stop drinking. When you nag, your chances of helping dwindle to nothing. In fact, your partner is likely to use it as an excuse to drink more. He or she will say you don't understand and may even start looking elsewhere for comfort.

If you have children, don't let your partner's alcoholism spoil your relationship with them. They need you. Also, don't drop old friends. They'll help you enjoy a full, useful life even though your partner is drinking.

We know people who are unafraid and even happy under these circumstances. Don't set your heart on reforming your partner. You probably can't do it.

These suggestions may be hard to follow, but they're likely to save you from heartbreak. A positive attitude on your part may prepare the way for a friendly discussion with your partner about his or her drinking. If your partner raises the topic of alcohol, don't be critical. Try instead to put yourself in his or her place. Show that you want to help.

You might tell your partner that you're worried and suggest that he or she look through this book—or at least read the descriptions of alcoholism in Chapters 2 and 3. You both need to understand the risks of continued heavy drinking. Show that you have faith in his or her ability to deal with the problem, and that your main concern is the partner's health and welfare.

If your partner isn't interested in discussing the matter, let it go. The subject will probably come up again on its own. Meanwhile, look for Alanon meetings in your area. This has helped the partners and families of many alcoholics, as well as the alcoholics themselves.

The partners of alcoholics in Category 2 should follow the same principles. But after a binge, these alcoholics should be asked if they really want to stop for good—not for their family but for themselves.

Many alcoholics are ready to change. If shown this book, they may realize that others understand their suffering. Alcoholics who are suspicious of the spiritual aspect of the program may be shown parts of the book that discuss its all-inclusive nature.

The support of a partner means a lot to the alcoholic who wants to recover. Problem drinkers who seem lukewarm or think they aren't alcoholic should probably be left alone. They shouldn't be pushed once the seed has been planted.

Most alcoholics are well aware that thousands of problem drinkers like them have recovered. But don't remind them of this after a binge, or you may trigger a resentment. Above all, don't hurry the person, for that will only delay recovery.

Alcoholics in Category 3 are the easiest to approach. When you're certain that your partner wants to stop, you can offer this book. The alcoholic may not share your enthusiasm, but he or she may read the book and try AA. If not, you probably won't have to wait long.

Don't pressure the alcoholic. Giving up liquor must be a personal decision. You may have to put up with more binges before recovery takes hold. Talk about alcoholism only when your partner raises the subject. If he or she is normal in other ways, the chances for recovery are good.

Alcoholics in Category 4 are often given up as hopeless. Many AA members who were this far gone when they joined the program have had spectacular recoveries. However, some are already too damaged to stop. Their alcoholism may be complicated by other health problems. In any case, a good doctor or psychiatrist should be consulted.

If your partner falls into Category 4, suggest that he or she read this book. If the person is already in an institution but is serious about recovery, there's still time. Of thousands of alcoholics released from hospitals and other institutions, those who join AA usually don't have to go back. Their Higher Power has restored them to good health.

Perhaps your partner is free but *should* be committed. Some people cannot or will not recover from alcoholism. When they become too dangerous to themselves or others, the kindest thing may be to consult a doctor about admitting them to a hospital. The families of these alcoholics suffer terribly, but not more than the alcoholics themselves.

You may have to start life over. Many partners of alcoholics have done this with happy results. Those who have adopted the spiritual program of Alanon have found their road much smoother.

The families of alcoholics often worry what others think, avoiding friends and relatives. They isolate themselves and imagine people are talking about them. They avoid the topic of alcoholism. When a couple has a family, the sober parent doesn't know how to explain the drinking parent's problem to the children.

You don't need to apologize for your partner as a person with weak character. He or she may be anything but. Without going into details, you can quietly let friends know the nature of your partner's illness—being careful not to reveal embarrassing details that might hurt the partner. This approach often opens up communication with friends and brings sympathy and understanding.

Your new courage and lack of self-consciousness will do wonders for you socially.

If you have children, try not to take sides in family arguments involving the drinking parent unless the children need protection. Use your energies to promote a better understanding all around. This can lessen the tension that grips the home of the problem drinker.

In the past, you may have made excuses for your partner's absences from work or social events. You probably used sickness as an excuse, when actually the person was drinking. Avoid such dishonesty. Your desire to protect the alcoholic shouldn't require you to lie to people who have a right to know the person's whereabouts. Let the partner explain.

When your partner is sober and in a good mood, he or she should be informed of your position, although you shouldn't show resentment for lies you've had to tell in the past. Ask your partner for suggestions about how to handle these situations in the future.

You may fear that your alcoholic partner will be fired, bringing shame on the family. It may have already happened. If so, it could be a blessing in disguise, convincing the person to stop drinking for good. You know from reading this book that alcoholics *can* stop with the help of a Higher Power.

Life is much better when lived on a spiritual basis. If the problems of the alcoholic can be solved by a Higher Power, so can yours. The families of alcoholics, like everybody else, often suffer from pride, self-pity, self-centeredness, and dishonesty. When the alcoholics whom we love start to apply spiritual principles to their lives, we, their partners, see that this approach can benefit us, too.

At first, some of us felt we didn't need help. We thought we were decent people, capable of better things if our partners would stop drinking. Were we too good to need a Higher Power?

Applying spiritual principles to our lives solves our problems, too—removing our fears, worries, and hurt feelings. We urge you to try Alanon. Nothing helps the alcoholic more than a changed attitude in the family.

If your partner is able to give up liquor, your life together is likely to be happy. But all your difficulties won't be solved at once. A seed has sprouted in new soil, and growth has just begun. There will be ups and downs. Many of the old conflicts will still be there. This is a fact of life.

Both of you will find your faith and sincerity tested. It's part of learning a new way to live. You'll make mistakes, but if you put forth an earnest effort, they won't drag you down. You'll profit from them and enjoy a better life.

Some of the snags that may lie ahead are irritation, hurt feelings, and resentment. The alcoholic sometimes becomes unreasonable. As the person's partner, you'll be tempted to be critical at times. A speck of disagreement can mushroom into a big argument. Arguments are dangerous for the alcoholic.

You might have to take responsibility for avoiding disputes or keeping them under control. This doesn't mean that you must agree with your partner when you have a difference of opinion. Just avoid being resentful or critical about it.

Surprisingly, the two of you will probably solve serious problems more easily than small ones. The next time you have a heated discussion, no matter what the subject, you should be able to say, "I'm sorry for getting so worked up. Let's talk about it again later."

Recovering alcoholics know that they owe their partners more than just giving up liquor. Most alcoholics genuinely want to make good. But old ways of thinking and behaving are the habits of years. If you can show your partner patience, tolerance, love and understanding, you're more likely to be treated the same way in return.

Many of us can describe exactly what kind of partner we'd like the alcoholic to be. It's natural to expect that when the drinking stops, the person will measure up to this ideal. This probably won't happen, at least for a while. Be patient. Spiritual development is a slow process.

As the partners of alcoholics, we may resent the fact that we couldn't cure the alcoholic—that a book or the support of other alcoholics could do in weeks what we tried to do for years.

Recovering alcoholics who follow a spiritual program often say that it was the devotion and care of their partners that brought them to the point where recovery was possible. Without you, your partner might have gone to pieces long ago.

As your partner gets more active in AA, you may be jealous of the time he or she spends with other alcoholics. You may resent your partner getting stirred up about other peoples' troubles but not yours. You've been starving for companionship, and now your partner passes long hours at AA meetings. You feel that your partner should belong to *you* again, not others.

The fact is that alcoholics need to work with fellow alcoholics to keep their sobriety. It's generally a mistake to discourage a partner's service work in AA. Your partner's excess enthusiasm is likely to tone down if you cooperate and don't complain. We suggest that you direct some of your time to the partners and families of other alcoholics through Alanon.

AA and Alanon encourage a sense of responsibility for others. Members learn to think more of what they can put into life than how much they can take out, and their lives become fuller as a result.

Probably you and your partner have been living alone too much. Isolation is a hallmark of alcoholism. You probably need fresh interests outside yourselves.

Your partner may make a good start in recovery, but just as things are looking up he or she comes home drunk. You needn't be alarmed, as long as you're satisfied that the person really wants to give up drinking. While it would be better if no relapse had occurred, it's not always a bad thing.

Alcoholics who "slip" must redouble their spiritual efforts. They don't need to be told that the relapse was regrettable. They know it. Alanon partners should cheer them up and ask how they can be more helpful.

The least hint of skepticism or criticism from you may lessen your partner's chances to recover. In a weak moment, he or she may use it as an excuse to drink.

Never try to remove the temptation of liquor from the alcoholic's life. Your slightest attempt to control the person's environment or affairs will be noticed. Alcoholics should be allowed to come and go as they please. This is important.

If the alcoholic gets drunk, you shouldn't take the blame. Your partner's craving for alcohol has either been relieved by a Higher Power or it hasn't. If it hasn't, it's better to know soon. Then the two of you can decide what needs to be done.

What we've described is based on experience, some of it painful. That's why we hope you can benefit from our mistakes and be spared learning some of these things the hard way.

Chapter 9

———

The Family Afterward

OUR SUGGESTIONS FOR LIVING WITH an alcoholic aren't intended to imply that the person should be handled with kid gloves. Family members should meet on the common ground of tolerance, understanding, and love. This requires some ego deflation all around.

Family members, including the alcoholic, probably have certain ideas about how they should relate to each other. Each wants to have his or her wishes respected. However, the more one person demands that the others give in, the more resentment may be created. This results in disagreements and unhappiness.

Why? Often each of them wants to be the leader. Family members may be trying to arrange the show to their own liking, unconsciously trying to see what they can take from family life rather than what they can give.

Living with an alcoholic for years is almost sure to make any husband, wife, or child neurotic. They all have some degree of spiritual illness. An alcoholic's abstinence from liquor is just the first step toward a happy, functional family.

Families should realize as they start this spiritual journey that the going won't always be smooth. They may get discouraged or be tempted to take short cuts along the way and get lost temporarily.

The families of alcoholics desire contentment and security. They remember when the drinker was a successful human being. They use yesterday's happiness as a yardstick for today. Then, when things don't measure up, they're unhappy.

After the alcoholic stops drinking, the family's confidence goes up. The good old days will soon be back, they think. Sometimes they demand that the ex-drinker bring them back at once. They believe that God owes this to them on a long-overdue account.

Most alcoholics have spent years pulling down their careers, relationships, and health. They need time to clear away the wreckage of the past. While old structures will eventually be replaced by new ones, years may be required to complete the process.

Alcoholics know they are to blame for damage to the family. It may take years of hard work for them to get back on their feet financially. But they shouldn't be criticized. Maybe they'll never have much money. It's wiser to appreciate them for what they're trying to become than for what they're trying to get.

The drinking careers of most alcoholics are marked by wild adventures. While some are humorous, many are shameful or tragic. The family's first impulse is to bury their skeletons in a closet. They may think their future happiness depends upon forgetting the past. We think this view conflicts with a better way of living.

Henry Ford said that experience is the thing of supreme value in life. This is true only if the past is turned to good account. We grow by our willingness to face past mistakes and turn them into assets. The alcoholic's past is actually an asset to the family. Sometimes it's almost the only one.

Families who are willing to talk about their painful history provide great support to other families damaged by alcoholism. We think that those who have been relieved of the ravages of the disease owe something to families who are still struggling.

When the occasion requires, the family in recovery should be willing to talk about their troubles, no matter how bad. Helping other families is part of the reason our lives are so rewarding now. When we follow the guidance of a Higher Power, the past is a precious possession. It's the key to a good life and happiness for others. With it, we can help them avoid much misery.

Of course, digging up past mistakes can also cause trouble and help no one. We know alcoholics who, in the flush of a spiritual experience, have told their partners about affairs they had while drinking. The partner may forgive the alcoholic at the time of the confession, but later bring the matter up in anger.

Some couples have separated because of such admissions until they could put hurt pride behind them. Usually, the alcoholic survives without a relapse, but not always. Unless some good purpose is served, affairs that occurred during the alcoholic's drinking days probably shouldn't be discussed.

The families of alcoholics find that keeping other kinds of secrets is usually a bad idea, however. So we share our stories. Outside of AA, this could be risky. People might laugh at us or use the information against us. Among the families of alcoholics, this rarely happens. The things we say about each other are almost always tempered by a spirit of love and tolerance.

A principle we live by is that we don't discuss the personal experiences of others unless we're sure they'd approve. It's better to stick to our own stories. We can criticize or laugh at ourselves without harm, but criticism or ridicule directed at others can be damaging.

Family members should be cautious about this. One careless, unkind remark can cause all kinds of trouble. We alcoholics are sensitive people. Some of us need a long time to outgrow this handicap.

Alcoholics tend to be enthusiastic and run to extremes. At the beginning of their journey, they may jump into life with great energy, delighted to get back on their feet. They may be so excited about their recovery that it's all they talk or think about. In either case, certain family problems are likely to arise.

When the alcoholic rushes to solve the family's financial difficulties, everyone is pleased at first. They think their money troubles will be over. But they're not so happy when they find themselves neglected.

The recovering alcoholic who works all day is tired at night. He or she may take little interest in the children and get irritated when reminded of it. These hard-working alcoholics may seem dull and boring, not happy and loving, the way their families want them to be. The family is disappointed and shows it.

Conflicts arise, because alcoholics who are trying hard to recover financially and socially often feel that they're doing quite well. The rest of the family may not agree. They were neglected and misused by the alcoholic in the past, and now they think they deserve more than they're getting. They want to be fussed over. They expect life to be happy again, the way it was before alcoholism took its toll.

The family wants the alcoholic to show remorse for the pain he or she caused. Instead, the ex-drinker may talk less and less and sometimes explode over small matters. The family is confused. They become critical and say that the person is falling down on his or her spiritual program. This situation can be avoided. Both sides may be partly right and partly wrong. Arguing only makes things worse.

The family must realize that the ex-drinker, though improved, is still healing. They should be thankful for the person's sobriety and ability to be active in the world again. The family should remember that drinking caused all kinds of damage that may take long to repair.

If they appreciate the progress the ex-drinker has made, they'll be less judgmental about occasional episodes of irritation, depression, or lack of interest in the family. These problems will fade when the family shows tolerance, love, and spiritual understanding.

On the other hand, the ex-drinker should remember that his or her alcoholism was mainly to blame for what happened to the family. Making up for this may take a lifetime. The alcoholic must also avoid the danger of concentrating too much on financial success. Although it's likely to come with continued sobriety, it shouldn't be top priority. For us, material success has followed spiritual progress, not the other way around.

Since family life has probably suffered more than anything, the alcoholic's energies should be directed toward making things right. Alcoholics who fail to show unselfishness and love in their homes aren't likely to get far in any direction. We know that some alcoholics have difficult husbands, wives, and children. However, the person who's recovering from alcoholism must remember that his or her actions did much to make the family that way.

As family members begin to admit their shortcomings, they lay the groundwork for cooperation. Family talks will help if they are held without heated argument, self-pity, self-justification, resentment, or criticism. Little by little, nondrinkers in the family will sense that they ask too much, while the recovering alcoholic will see that he or she gives too little. Giving rather than getting will become the guiding principle.

Some alcoholics have a powerful spiritual experience as soon as they quit drinking. Overnight they're different people. They may become so religious that they can't focus on anything else. The partner and children may get annoyed at the alcoholic's talk of spiritual matters morning, noon, and night.

Some alcoholics demand that the family, too, must find God. Or they tell those who are already religious that they don't know what it's all about. The family is told that they'd better get the right brand of spirituality while there's still time.

The family may feel jealous because the alcoholic's new Higher Power seems to have replaced them. While they're grateful that drinking is out of the picture, they may not like the idea that God has performed a miracle where they failed.

They can't understand why their devotion didn't cure the alcoholic, forgetting that the person was beyond human aid. The ex-drinker isn't so spiritual after all, they say. If the alcoholic means to make amends for past wrongs, why does everyone but the family get his or her attention? They suspect that the ex-drinker has gone off the deep end.

Alcoholics who preach to their families aren't as off-balance as they seem. Many of us have felt intoxicated by our newly discovered Higher Power. Like a starving prospector whose pick has struck gold, we were joyous at being released from a lifetime of frustration.

Ex-drinkers have struck something better than gold and may hold the new treasure close for a time. They haven't yet realized that their discovery will continue to pay off only if they keep passing it on to others.

At the same time, they'll soon see that a life that leaves the family out isn't really spiritual. If families understand that the alcoholic's feverish activities are just a phase, all will be well. When the family is sympathetic, spiritual growing pains disappear.

On the other hand, alcoholics with critical families often retreat into silence, feeling they've earned the right. For years, their drinking put them on the wrong side of every argument. But now they feel that God is on their side. If the family continues to find fault, the ex-drinker may withdraw even more instead of joining the family in a healthy way.

Families should let recovering alcoholics find their own path. Even when ex-drinkers are slack in their family obligations, they should be given free rein in helping other alcoholics. This does more to ensure early sobriety than anything else. Alcoholics who reach out to others are less likely to drink again than those who put their careers or financial success first.

Some of us lived in a world of spiritual make-believe at the beginning of sobriety. We later replaced this dream world with a sense of purpose and awareness of a Higher Power. While it's all right for our heads to be in the clouds in a spiritual sense, our feet must be firmly planted on the ground as we go through our days. There's no conflict between a powerful spiritual experience and a sane, happy life.

Whether the family has spiritual beliefs or not, they should be aware of the principles that the ex-drinker is trying to live by. They can hardly fail to approve of them, even when they aren't practiced perfectly. Nothing helps the alcoholic who gets off track spiritually more than a family who adopts a sane spiritual program and applies it in practical ways.

As alcoholics return to normal and become more assertive, it can mean trouble unless the family is on guard and can make friendly compromises. When liquor still ruled the lives of these alcoholics, their drinking placed them constantly in the wrong. Their partners made the plans and gave orders. The drinker was treated like a sick person or a naughty child.

Drinking tends to isolate families from the outside world. Most alcoholics drop normal activities such as volunteer work, clubs, and hobbies. When the ex-drinker takes these activities up again, the family may get jealous. They may feel that they deserve the full attention of the recovering alcoholic. Instead of trying some new outlets themselves, they may demand that the person stay home and make up for lost time.

From the outset, family members should face the fact that everyone must compromise if the family is to enjoy harmony. The ex-drinker will need to spend time with fellow alcoholics, but other activities are also necessary for a balanced life. The alcoholic and family should make new friends, get involved in community work, and take time for spiritual pursuits.

Alcoholics who once made fun of religion may change their minds about involvement in a church, synagogue, or other spiritual institution. They may discover that they have much in common with the people in these settings. While they may not agree on every point with others, it's a way to make new friends and find fresh avenues of usefulness and pleasure. However, this is only a suggestion. Each person must make his or her own choices about spiritual activity.

We've been talking of serious, sometimes tragic matters. But we aren't a glum lot. If newcomers could see no joy in the way we live, they wouldn't want the AA program. We insist on getting pleasure from life. We avoid becoming gloomy over world affairs and don't carry the troubles of society on our shoulders.

When we see someone sinking into the pit of alcoholism, we offer what we have to share. We tell our own painful stories to show that we've been through similar experiences. But we don't take on the entire burden of other alcoholics, for we'd soon be overwhelmed if we did.

We believe in laughter and a cheerful attitude. Outsiders are sometimes shocked when we chuckle over what seems to be a tragic story. Why shouldn't we laugh? We've recovered and have been given the power to help others.

Sick people and those who never have fun don't laugh much. So each family should enjoy life together as much as they can. We were meant to be happy, joyous, and free—not filled with sorrow as we once were.

It's clear that we caused our own misery, and it wasn't the fault of some Higher Power. If trouble comes to us during sobriety, we take advantage of the chance to tap our spiritual resources and call on the goodness of our Higher Power.

Now a word about health. A body damaged by alcohol recovers slowly. Twisted thinking and depression don't vanish in the blink of an eye. On the other hand, our spiritual way of life is a powerful tonic. We who have recovered from serious drinking are often models of mental health. We've seen great improvement in our physical health, too. Few of us show the ravages of alcoholism.

This doesn't mean that we ignore our health. Most of us have access to skilled doctors, therapists, and other professionals. We don't hesitate to consult them about any health problems we may have. Although we count on our Higher Power to work miracles in our lives, we don't discount the importance of good doctors and therapists. Alcoholics at all stages of recovery often benefit from their services.

A doctor who reviewed this book before publication told us that sweets are often helpful to recovering alcoholics. He recommended that they keep chocolate on hand for quick energy when they're tired. He added that occasional night cravings could be satisfied by candy. Many of us have found this to be true.

During our drinking days, some of us overindulged in sex. Couples are occasionally disappointed to find that without alcohol the ex-drinker has trouble having satisfactory sex. Unless the reason is understood, emotional upset may result. Some of us have gone through this, only to enjoy even better intimacy within a few months. Couples shouldn't hesitate to consult a doctor or therapist if a problem persists.

Re-establishing friendly relations with their children may be difficult for some alcoholics. The minds of young children are greatly affected when an alcoholic parent is drinking heavily. Without saying so, they may secretly hate the person for the harm done to them and to the other parent.

Sometimes, the children become hard and cynical. They can't forgive and forget. They may cling to this attitude long after the ex-drinker's new way of living and thinking has been accepted by the other parent.

In time, the children will see that the alcoholic parent is becoming a new person, and their attitude will change. They can then be invited to join in meditations and family discussions. From that point on, progress is likely to be rapid, with heartwarming results.

Whether the family adopts a spiritual way of life or not, the alcoholic must do so in order to recover. Family members must be convinced of the person's commitment beyond the shadow of a doubt. Seeing is believing to most families who have lived with a problem drinker.

Criticism of the alcoholic often backfires. One of our members was a heavy smoker and coffee drinker. Certainly he overindulged. Meaning to be helpful, his wife scolded him about it. He admitted he was overdoing cigarettes and coffee, but he wasn't ready to stop. His wife, a person who thought these habits were unhealthy and immoral, nagged him. She finally drove him to a fit of anger, and he got drunk.

Of course, his reaction was wrong, as he admitted afterward. After mending his spiritual fences, he became a highly effective member of AA. He still smokes and drinks coffee, but his wife no longer judges him. She recognizes that she was mistaken in making a big issue of these habits when the disease of alcoholism was rapidly being cured.

We have three mottoes: "First things first," "Live and let live," and "Easy does it."

Chapter 10

———

To Employers

A FRIEND WHO HAS HIRED and fired hundreds of employees described his experience with problem drinkers in the workplace.

"I was once the assistant manager of a company employing over six thousand people. One day my secretary told me that a Mr. Smith wanted to talk with me on the phone. I had warned Smith, a heavy drinker, that he had just one more chance. Not long afterward, he called me two days in a row so drunk he could hardly talk. I told him that he was fired.

"My secretary said it wasn't *that* Mr. Smith. It was his brother. I still expected an appeal, but the brother said, 'I called to tell you that Paul jumped from a hotel window last Saturday. He left a note saying that you were the best boss he ever had, and that you weren't to blame in any way.'

"Another time, a newspaper clipping fell out of a letter I'd opened at my desk. It was the death notice of one of my best employees. After a two-week binge, he'd placed his toe on the trigger of a loaded shotgun, with the barrel in his mouth. I'd let him go for drinking six weeks earlier.

"In another case, the wife of an employee called asking whether his life insurance was still good. Four days earlier he'd hanged himself in his woodshed. I'd had to dismiss him for drinking even though he was a brilliant worker—one of the best I'd ever had. Because I didn't understand alcoholism as I do now, three talented human beings were lost to this world.

"What irony! I later became an alcoholic myself. I would have killed myself, too, except for the help of an understanding person. My alcoholism cost the company huge amounts of money. Training people for responsible positions is a big investment. This kind of waste goes on everywhere, but might be reduced if we knew more about alcoholism."

It's easy to see why employers have been ineffective in dealing with problem drinkers. To them, alcoholics may seem like first-rate fools. But because the employer values certain people's abilities or has a special liking for them, they are kept on much longer than others with the same problem. Some employers have tried almost every remedy they can think of. Worn down by the effort, they can hardly be blamed for letting alcoholic employees go.

A bank officer told me about a manager at his bank who had all the symptoms of alcoholism. This seemed like a chance for me to be helpful, so I spent two hours talking to him about alcoholics. His comment was, "Very interesting, but I'm sure this man is through drinking. He just came from three months' leave of absence and looks fine. Besides, the board of directors told him this was his last chance."

All I could say was that if the man followed the usual pattern, things would get worse. Why not introduce him to AA and give him a real chance? I pointed out that I'd had no alcohol for three years. I often faced trouble that would have sent nine of ten people back to the bottle. Why not at least let this man hear my story?

"Oh, no," said my banker friend. "This fellow is either through with liquor or he's out of a job. If he has your willpower and guts, he'll make it."

I wanted to throw up my hands in frustration. I'd failed to make my friend understand. He couldn't accept that his employee suffered from a serious illness. There was nothing to do but wait.

Sure enough, the man did slip and was fired. When we contacted him, he said he was ready to accept our program. He is now on the road to recovery.

To me, the bank officer's handling of the matter reflected a lack of knowledge about alcoholism often found among employers. Their attitude prevents them from learning how to save valuable employees.

If you supervise problem drinkers in your workplace, you may have some fixed ideas about alcoholism whether you drink or not. If you're a moderate drinker, you may have less patience with alcoholics than nondrinkers do. Being able to drink now and then without ill effects, you may have opinions about how liquor affects people. After all, you can take it or leave it.

Perhaps you can get tipsy on occasion and go to work the next day with no problem. You may think that people who can't do the same thing are weak or stupid. Even when you understand the disease better, you might find it hard to let go of your old ideas.

A look at alcoholics in your organization may be revealing. Don't they tend to be fast, creative thinkers with likable personalities? When sober, don't they work hard and get things done on time? Wouldn't they be highly valued employees if they didn't drink? Perhaps they should be given the same consideration as other employees who suffer from an illness.

If you believe that problem drinking is simply a bad habit or a vice caused by a stubborn nature or a weak will, read Chapters 2 and 3 in this book. They describe the features of alcoholism in detail.

If you can accept the idea that alcoholism is a disease, can you forgive the employee's mistakes of the past? Can you see the problem drinker as a victim of abnormal thinking caused by the effects of alcohol?

Physicians report that the spinal fluid pressure of an alcoholic can rise so high that it ruptures brain tissue. No wonder alcoholics aren't rational! Normal drinkers don't suffer these consequences. Because they have few ill effects from drinking, they can't understand why the alcoholic does.

Alcoholic employees who go out on a binge usually try to hide their drunken behavior the next day. You may find it hard to understand how upright people could get into so much trouble. They have a gift for finding themselves in messy situations. They may be models of good character when sober but behave disgracefully when drunk. Afterward, they are truly sorry. Their alcoholic behavior is generally caused by the abnormal effects of alcohol on their brains.

Almost always, the outrageous behaviors of alcoholics are temporary. Not always, of course. They may be dishonest people to begin with. If so, they may take advantage of you when they sense your desire to understand and help.

Employees whose actions show that they don't want to stop drinking may as well be fired, and the sooner the better. You're not doing them a favor by keeping them. In fact, being fired may be a blessing in disguise, giving the drinker a needed jolt.

In my own case, nothing my company could have done would have stopped my drinking. As long as I could hang onto my job, I didn't have to face how serious my problem was. If they'd fired me first and then taken the trouble to help me find the solution described in this book, I might have returned to work six months later, a well person.

There are many people who sincerely want to give up alcohol. With them you can go far. Your understanding will yield dividends. If you know such employees and wish to help, it usually pays off, if only as a matter of good business. By understanding that alcoholism is a mental and physical illness, you may be able to overlook a worker's poor performance of the past. Here are some suggestions for helping an employee with a drinking problem.

Tell the person that you're aware of the situation and that it must stop. You might express your appreciation for his or her abilities but indicate that dismissal will be necessary if the drinking continues. A firm attitude at this point is often helpful.

You can assure the employee that you don't intend to lecture or find fault. Say that if you made this error in the past, it was from a lack of understanding. You have no hard feelings. You might share what you have learned about the disease of alcoholism as a serious and sometimes fatal illness.

Ask whether the employee has a desire to recover. Is this person prepared to take every step necessary to get well, to stop drinking for good? Problem drinkers should be questioned carefully about their sincerity.

Some employees try to deceive themselves or their employers about their desire to recover. You should make certain that this isn't happening. When the problem drinkers you interview say they want to quit, do they mean it? Or deep down are they trying to fool you? Do they secretly hope that some day they'll be able to have an occasional drink?

When employees are vague about the issue and hint that maybe they'll be able to drink normally at some time in the future, you might as well discharge them after the next binge—which they're sure to have. They should understand this clearly. Either you're dealing with a person who can and will recover or you aren't. If you're not, why waste everyone's time?

After you're satisfied that the employee wants to give up alcohol and will go to any length to do so, suggest a course of action. You may want to mention this book. Also, you might tell the person that most active alcoholics can benefit from a certain amount of medical treatment at first. In fact, in some cases it's essential. This should be decided by a doctor.

Whatever treatment method is used, the mind and body must be cleared of the effects of alcohol before true recovery can begin. Most alcoholics do better in a treatment setting where they can think straight again and get over their craving for liquor.

If you propose treatment, it may be necessary for the company to pay for it or advance the cost and deduct it from later paychecks. The person should feel personally responsible for his or her recovery.

If the alcoholic accepts your offer, you should point out that treatment is only a part of the picture. In addition to getting the best possible medical care, the employee must undergo a change of heart—a transformed attitude and a new way of thinking. We alcoholics must place recovery above all else, for without it we lose everything.

Are you reasonably confident of the employee's ability to recover? Can you keep the person's problem confidential, agreeing never to discuss it with others without his or her consent? This issue of confidentiality may be best raised when the employee returns to work.

Some employers won't agree with all the ideas in this book. While we may not have the last word on the subject, what we've described has certainly worked for us. After all, isn't a positive outcome more important than the method used to achieve it?

Problem drinkers who undergo treatment learn the grim truth about alcoholism whether they like it or not. The truth won't hurt them a bit, even though it may be hard to take at first. If they're given this book, they shouldn't be ordered to abide by its suggestions. They must decide for themselves.

You hope that their new knowledge about alcoholism will do the trick. It may or may not. If the patient's physician isn't familiar with the treatment of alcoholism, you might offer to share this book.

Your persistence should bring gratifying successes among your employees. Since AA has become more widely known, groups have sprung up in countless places, so most people can find meetings to attend. Meanwhile, the book alone may help considerably.

Employees returning to work after treatment should be interviewed about the experience. Do they think they've found the answer to their drinking problem? Employees who are frank with you and believe you'll accept whatever they reveal to you are probably off to a good start in their recovery.

It's important to remain calm if an employee reveals disturbing personal secrets. Perhaps the person has padded an expense account or stolen from the company. The AA program of recovery demands rigorous honesty. Can you write off the person's mistakes as you would a bad account and start over? If the employee owes the company money, arrangements can be made for repayment.

Employees who talk about their home situations or other problems outside of work may benefit from helpful suggestions. They should be able to talk frankly, as long as they don't involve fellow employees in their disclosures. If your attitude is warm and accepting, you'll be rewarded with the employee's loyalty.

The greatest enemies of alcoholics are resentment, jealousy, frustration, and fear. Wherever people gather together in business settings, there will be rivalry and competition. One can't escape workplace politics entirely. Sometimes alcoholics get the idea that people are trying to put them down when it's not the case. But the reality is that some employees may use the drinking histories of their co-workers against them at times.

In one case, we were told of a malicious co-worker of a recovering alcoholic who was always making little jokes about the person's drinking adventures. This was a sneaky way of tattling on the person.

In another case, only a few people knew about an alcoholic employee being sent to a treatment center. A short time after the person returned to work, the news was all over the company. Naturally, this harmed the person's chances of recovery. Often, the employer can protect employees trying to build a new life from this kind of talk, defending them against unfair criticism.

Alcoholics are generally energetic people. They work hard and play hard. Employees who return to work after treatment try to make good. They may overdo, failing to recognize the physical and mental adjustments required to live without alcohol. You should discourage these employees from working long hours and suggest that they enjoy some leisure time.

Employees active in AA usually want to help other problem drinkers. Occasionally this activity requires some hours away from work. Allowing a reasonable amount of time for service work is helpful, because reaching out to other alcoholics is necessary to maintain sobriety.

An employee who has quit drinking for several months may be glad to help a co-worker who has a drinking problem, provided the person is willing to cooperate. An alcoholic who no longer drinks can talk to another alcoholic, even one in a higher position, without ever taking advantage of the situation.

In general, you can trust recovering alcoholics. If the person's spouse calls you saying that he or she is at home sick, you might suspect that drinking is the reason. If this is the case but the employee is really trying to recover, you'll be told the truth even if there's a good chance of the person being fired.

Recovering alcoholics know they must be honest if they're to live worthwhile lives. They appreciate having the trust of others who aren't trying to run their lives or shield them from the temptation to drink. Most recovering alcoholics can be relied upon in any setting.

When employees stumble even once, you'll have to decide whether to dismiss them. If they don't appear serious about recovery, there's no doubt that you should. On the other hand, if you're sure they're doing their best, you may want to give them a second chance. But you shouldn't feel you have to, for your obligation has already been met.

If your organization is large, you might want to give your managers a copy of this book. Let them know that you have no quarrel with alcoholic employees who want to recover.

Managers who supervise problem drinkers are often in a tough position, especially when the people are their friends. They gloss matters over when alcoholic behavior becomes a problem, hoping the situation will improve. They may even risk their own positions by helping a drinker who should have been discharged long ago—or else given a chance at treatment.

Managers can offer this book to problem drinkers and ask whether they'd like to quit. They should point out that people drinking on the job put them on the spot. The organization realizes that alcoholism is an illness and wants to offer help to employees who are interested. For those who are sent to treatment, past problems will be overlooked as long as they abstain from alcohol when they return. Otherwise, they'll be asked to resign or be dismissed.

Managers who disagree with the ideas in this book should probably not use it with their employees. But they should at least read enough to learn more about alcoholism and how to handle problem drinkers at work. It will help them act fairly and stop covering up for alcoholic employees.

No one should be fired because of alcoholism without being given a chance at recovery. Problem drinkers who want to stop should be given a chance. Only if they cannot stop or don't want to should they be dismissed. There are few exceptions.

This approach allows good employees to be rehabilitated. The employer may dismiss those who continue drinking and do it with a clear conscience. The problem of alcoholism is costly in terms of time, money, reputation, and human resources. It's sensible to stop this waste, while at the same time giving valuable employees a chance to make good.

When one officer of an industrial company was approached by a member of AA about the problem of alcoholism in the workplace, he said, "I'm glad you fellows were able to quit drinking. But our company policy is not to interfere with employees' habits. Workers who drink so much that their jobs suffer are fired. I don't see how

AA can help us, for we don't have a problem with alcoholism."

This company spends millions on research every year. They provide employee benefits and recreational facilities. They're interested in their employees' welfare. But alcoholism? They don't think it's a problem.

Maybe this attitude is typical. We've often seen it in business. The man we talked to might be shocked to learn the cost of alcoholism to his company each year. Managers seldom realize how far-reaching the problem is. If you think your organization has no alcoholics, keep your eyes open. You might be surprised.

Of course, alcoholic employees should not receive undue time and attention or be treated with favoritism. Employees who really want to recover don't desire special treatment. Far from it. They'll work hard and be grateful for the help they're given.

Today I own a small company and employ two recovering alcoholics. They produce as much as five normal people. And why not? They have a new attitude, and they've been saved from a living death. I've enjoyed helping them get sober.

Chapter 11

—

A Vision for You

Normal people drink to enjoy themselves with friends as a harmless escape from cares, boredom, and worry. It's a chance to enjoy life.

This isn't true for alcoholics in their last days of heavy drinking. The good times are over. They want desperately to enjoy life the way they used to. They are obsessed with the idea that some new miracle of willpower will make it possible. But when they try to drink normally again, they fail.

Ruled by King Alcohol, they live on the edge of insanity. The less willing people are to put up with their drinking, the more they isolate themselves. The chill of loneliness makes their lives bleaker every day.

Some go to bad neighborhoods and cheap bars for company. The first few drinks are fun, but as the binges continue, blackouts begin. These drinkers awaken to feelings of fear, confusion, frustration, and depression. Unhappy alcoholics who read this will understand.

Sometimes a serious drinker who's stayed sober a short time will say, "I don't miss it at all. Feel better. Work better. Having a better time."

We know that this can be whistling in the dark. People who fool themselves would give anything to take half a dozen drinks and get away with it. They may quit for a while, but soon they're back to the bottle. In reality, they aren't happy with their sobriety. They can't picture life without alcohol. Eventually, they won't be able to imagine life with or without it. Then they will know true loneliness and wish for the end.

You may say, "I'm willing to try this program. But won't my life be boring and gloomy without alcohol? I don't want to live like some of the self-righteous people I see. I know I have to give up liquor, but how can I? Can you offer a good substitute?"

Yes, and it's much better. It's the fellowship of Alcoholic Anonymous. There you'll find release from care, boredom, and worry. Your imagination will come to life. Your existence will finally take on meaning. Your best years lie ahead. In AA you'll find friends and a feeling of togetherness, just as we did.

"How?" you may ask.

As you begin your recovery in AA, you'll meet other suffering alcoholics. All kinds of people are waiting for the relief AA can give them. Among them, you may find lifelong friends. You'll forge a bond that comes from escaping a common disaster. You'll discover what it means to help others so they can survive and find a good life, too. You'll learn the meaning of "Love thy neighbor as thyself."

It may seem incredible that suffering alcoholics can return to happy, useful lives. How can they recover from such deep misery, get back their reputations, and regain hope? Since it's happened to you, it can happen to them. If you're willing to share your experience and welcome them to the program, they're likely to come. Miracles still happen. We are proof of that.

Our hope is that desperate alcoholics around the world will see what this book has to offer and follow its suggestions. Given the chance, many will follow our path. As they recover, they will reach out to other alcoholics, so that AA groups will spring up everywhere as safe havens for those seeking a cure for this disease.

If you've already helped several families adopt our way of life, you may want to take our work further. The best way to give you a glimpse of your future may be to tell you about the early years of AA.

In 1935, one of us went on a business trip that turned out badly. If he'd been successful, he would have been set on his feet financially. But his business deal ended in a bitter lawsuit and there were hard feelings all around.

He found himself almost broke and his reputation ruined. He'd been sober only a few months, was still physically weak, and knew he was in danger. He wanted to talk with someone, but he was a stranger in town.

He paced his hotel lobby one afternoon worrying about how he'd pay his bill. At one end was a church directory. At the other was a cozy bar full of people laughing and talking. There he could escape his worries and loneliness. But without something to drink, he might not have the courage to start up a conversation, and he'd have to spend the weekend alone.

He knew he couldn't drink, but why not order a bottle of ginger ale and hope someone would join him? He'd been sober for six months. Maybe he could handle just two or three drinks. He was on thin ice.

The old insanity was creeping back—the belief that it would be okay to have that first drink. With a shiver, he walked back to the church directory. He could still hear music and laughter from the bar.

He remembered his family. And he thought about the suffering alcoholics who might die because there was no one to help them recover. There were probably many in the town where he was staying. He decided to phone one of the churches listed in the lobby, and his sanity returned. He thanked his Higher Power and placed the call.

The minister who answered the phone told him about a man in town who was once respected and successful. But alcohol brought him down. He owed money and was in danger of losing his home. His wife was ill, and his children were angry with him.

The man was desperate to stop drinking but couldn't, the minister said. He'd tried many times. He realized something was wrong with him, but he understood nothing about alcoholism.

When the two met, the desperate man admitted that no amount of willpower could stop his drinking for long. He knew that he'd have to have a spiritual experience but couldn't bring himself to seek it.

He said he dreaded being found out. Like many other alcoholics, he believed that his drinking was a secret. If he confessed, he was afraid he'd lose what was left of his business, and this would bring more distress to his family. He just couldn't do that, he said.

After their evening together, the man felt he was getting control of his drinking. But then he went on a roaring drunk. This time, he saw that he'd have to put his drinking problem in the hands of a Higher Power.

One morning, he took the bull by the horns and told others about his alcoholism. To his surprise, they received him warmly. He learned that many of them were already aware of his drinking problem. He made the rounds of people he had hurt, even though he feared that his confession might end his career.

Returning home that night, he was tired but happy. The man has not had a drink since then. He now means a great deal to the people in his community. The damages done by thirty years of hard drinking were repaired in four years.

Our friend and this man became friends. Both saw they had to stay active in their spiritual program to remain sober. They called the head nurse at a local hospital and explained their need to work with other alcoholics. Did she have anyone who needed help?

She said, "We sure have! A man here just assaulted a couple of nurses. He goes crazy when he's drinking. He's a good fellow when he's sober, even though he's been in here eight times in the last six months. He used to be a well-known lawyer in town. Right now he's strapped in a bed."

Here was a prospect for the two friends, although it didn't sound promising. The spiritual program of AA wasn't as well understood as it is now. They asked the nurse to put the man in a private room, and they'd come to see him. When they arrived at the man's room, he said, "Who are you guys, and why this private room? I've always been put in a ward before."

The visitors said, "We're here to give you help for your alcoholism."

The man's face made it clear that he felt hopeless. He said, "It's no use. Nothing could fix me. The last three times I was here, I got drunk on the way home from the hospital. I'm afraid to go out the door. I can't understand it."

For an hour, the two friends talked to the man about their drinking experiences. They described how liquor poisons the mind and body of the alcoholic. They talked about the twisted thinking that leads to the first drink. Over and over, the man said, "That's me. That's me. I drink like that."

"You know what you're talking about, but I don't see what good it will do," said the sick man. "You're both worth something. I'm not. I'm a nobody now. From what you tell me, I'm more convinced than ever that I can't stop."

At this, the visitors burst out laughing. The man said, "Damn little to laugh about that I can see."

Then the two friends told about their spiritual experiences. They described the program of action that they'd followed.

The man said, "I once attended church, but that didn't fix me. On the mornings I was hung over, I prayed and swore I'd never touch another drop. In a couple of hours I'd be drunk again."

When the visitors returned the next day, they found the man more open to what they had to say. He'd been thinking it over. "Maybe you're right," he said. "God should be able to do anything." Then he added, "He sure didn't do much for me when I was trying to fight liquor on my own."

On the third visit, the lawyer turned his life over to the care of his Creator and vowed to do whatever was necessary to stay sober. His wife hardly dared to have hope, although she thought she saw a change in him. He was beginning to have a spiritual experience.

That afternoon, the man walked out of the hospital a free man. A short time later, he ran for office and gave political speeches. His campaign often took him where liquor was served.

Sometimes he was up all night. He lost the election by a small margin but he found a Higher Power. In doing this, he found himself.

This happened in June 1935. The man never drank again. He became a respected member of his community. He helped others recover from alcoholism and became active in his church, which he hadn't attended for years.

So you see, there were three alcoholics in that town who felt they had to share what they'd found or they'd be sunk. They failed with a few prospects, but then a fourth man turned up. He'd been sent by a friend who'd heard about AA's success with problem drinkers.

He was a carefree guy whose parents couldn't decide whether he wanted to stop drinking or not. Being religious, they were shocked that their son refused to attend church. He suffered from his binges, but it seemed that nothing could be done for him. He did agree, though, to go to the hospital. There he was put in the same room where the lawyer had stayed.

After talking with his three AA visitors for a bit, the young man said, "The way you guys talk about this spiritual stuff makes sense. I'm ready to try it. I guess my parents were right after all." So one more person was added to the AA fellowship.

When our friend from the hotel lobby returned home after a long absence, he and the other founders of AA knew that they must help other alcoholics in order to stay sober themselves. Dedicating themselves to others was one of the best rewards of sobriety. They shared their homes and resources, gladly giving their spare time to twelfth step work. At any time of day or night, they were ready to talk to suffering alcoholics.

The fellowship gradually grew. There were a few upsetting failures, but in such cases the alcoholic's family was invited into the program's spiritual way of living. Even if the alcoholic couldn't be helped, the family could be relieved of some worry and suffering.

A year and six months after the program began, the founders had succeeded with seven more alcoholics. They saw a lot of each other. Most nights, men and women met at one of their homes. Happy to be released from alcoholism, the founders of AA were always thinking of how they could share their discovery with newcomers.

These were closed meetings, which only people who were admitted alcoholics could attend. However, the group also set aside one night a week to welcome anyone interested in learning about the AA way of life. Their main goal was to provide a time and place where people could bring their problems.

Outsiders got interested in the fellowship. One couple opened their large home to AA. Eventually they became so involved in the work that they devoted their residence to it. Many discouraged spouses of alcoholics found understanding people at those early AA meetings whose partners were also alcoholics. They could talk with others who were in the same boat, hear their stories, and get advice on how to handle the alcoholic who was still drinking.

Many alcoholics just out of the hospital found freedom in that house. They couldn't resist the happy atmosphere and the people who laughed at their problems and understood newcomers so well.

On one visit to the couple's house, the man in our story listened to a recovering alcoholic whose experience was much like his own. The happy expressions on the faces of the people in the house and the stimulating atmosphere told him he'd found a place where he belonged.

He was drawn by the practical approach to personal problems, the tolerant attitudes of the people, and the informal atmosphere. He loved the feeling of standing on common ground with them and basking in the amazing understanding they showed.

He and his wife were inspired by the chance to help alcoholics and their families. They made new friends—people they somehow felt they'd always known. They found a benevolent and all-powerful Higher Power.

In a few years, the house could barely hold its visitors. After a while, there were sixty to eighty people there each week. Alcoholics came from near and far. Families drove long distances to attend. In 1939, an AA founder wrote, "We think that some day our fellowship will number many hundreds." *[AA now has more than 2 million members.]*

Life in Alcoholics Anonymous goes beyond attending meetings and doing twelfth step work. It also involves helping the families of alcoholics. Angry parents may want to know why their children drink. Some newly sober alcoholics need assistance finding jobs and getting on their feet financially. We give this kind of help when it's justified.

No newcomer has sunk too low to be welcomed to the fellowship if he or she means business. Social differences, resentments, and petty irritations are shrugged off and laughed at because we are united on our spiritual journey. We were all on the same sinking ship, rescued by a miracle. We devote ourselves to the welfare of others and find that many things that once worried us no longer matter.

As AA groups in the Midwest grew, they also formed in Eastern cities. One city even had a well-known hospital for the treatment of alcohol and drug addiction. Many alcoholics felt the presence of a Higher Power there for the first time in their lives. Early members of AA were grateful to the head doctor for his belief in Alcoholics Anonymous.

Every few days, this doctor would recommend the AA program to a patient. Because he understood our work, he could select alcoholics with the potential to recover on a spiritual basis. AA groups formed in the city and grew rapidly. Close friendships and a spirit of helping others were central features of those groups.

Some day we hope that all alcoholics who travel will find AA meetings in the cities and towns they visit. Often new groups are started because AA members have imported the fellowship from other places. Recovering alcoholics drop in at meetings far from home whenever they can. In this way, they lend a helping hand and at the same time avoid temptation on the road.

Even if there are no meetings near your home, this book will give you what you need to begin your recovery. You may think, "I'm too nervous and alone. I can't do it." But you can. By tapping a source of power greater than yourself, being patient and willing, and working hard at the program, you can succeed just as we have.

One AA member who moved to a big city found that it probably contained more alcoholics per square mile than any other place in the country. He contacted a well-known psychiatrist who'd become interested in mental health problems in the community. The doctor was open to any new method that might help alcoholics. The doctor asked our friend's advice.

After learning about the AA program, the doctor decided to try it with some patients. In addition, the chief psychiatrist of an inner city hospital agreed to find prospects among the alcoholics living in poverty and despair who came for treatment.

Soon this AA member had many new friends. Some sank back into their miserable living conditions, but many got sober. He foresaw that when recovering alcoholics discovered the joy of helping others face life again, there would be no stopping them. They would make sure that the suffering alcoholics around them were given the chance to recover, too.

The reader may say, "But I won't have the benefit of contact with the people who wrote this book." You can never be sure whose path you'll cross in recovery. Remember that your real reliance must be on your Higher Power, who can show you how to find the fellowship you seek.

This book was written only to make suggestions. There's a lot we don't know. Your Higher Power will reveal more to you over time.

In the morning, pray to see what you can do to help the alcoholic who still drinks. If your life is in order, the answers will come. But you can't give away what you don't have. Be sure your relationship with your Higher Power is solid, and wonderful things will happen—a wonderful truth for us.

Give yourself to the God of your understanding. Admit your faults to your Higher Power and those close to you. Clear away the wreckage of your past. Join the fellowship and give freely of what you've found. We'll be with you in spirit, and you'll surely meet some of us as you trudge the road of happy destiny.

Appendix I

The Twelve Steps

1. We admitted that we were powerless over alcohol and our lives had become unmanageable.
2. We came to believe that a Power greater than ourselves could restore us to sanity.
3. We made a decision to turn our will and our lives over to the care of a Higher Power of our understanding.
4. We made a searching and fearless moral inventory of ourselves.
5. We admitted to our Higher Power, to ourselves, and to another human being the exact nature of our wrongs.
6. We were entirely ready to have our Higher Power remove all these defects of character.
7. We humbly asked our Higher Power to remove our shortcomings.
8. We made a list of all persons we had harmed and became willing to make amends to them all.
9. We made direct amends to such people wherever possible, except when to do so would injure them or others.
10. We continued to take personal inventory and when we were wrong promptly admitted it.
11. We sought through prayer and meditation to improve our conscious contact with the Higher Power of our understanding, asking only for guidance and the willingness to follow it.
12. Having had a spiritual awakening as the result of these steps, we tried to carry this message to alcoholics and to practice these principles in all our affairs.

Appendix II

The Twelve Traditions

1. Our common welfare should come first. Personal recovery depends upon AA unity.
2. For our group purpose there is only one final authority—a Higher Power as expressed in our group conscience. Our leaders are but trusted servants. They do not govern.
3. The only requirement for AA membership is a desire to stop drinking.
4. Each AA group should be independent except in matters affecting other groups or AA as a whole.
5. Each group has but one primary purpose—to carry its message to the alcoholic who still suffers.
6. An AA group ought never endorse, finance or lend the AA name to any related facility or outside enterprise, lest problems of money, property and prestige divert us from our primary purpose.
7. Every AA group should be fully self-supporting, taking no outside contributions.
8. AA should remain forever nonprofessional, but our service centers may employ special workers.
9. AA as such ought never be organized, but we may create service boards or committees directly responsible to those they serve.
10. AA has no opinion on outside issues. The AA name ought never be drawn into public controversy.
11. Our public relations policy is based on attraction rather than promotion. We need always maintain personal anonymity at the level of the press and other media.
12. Anonymity is the spiritual foundation of all our Traditions, always reminding us to place principles before personalities.

Appendix III

Dr. Bob's Story

[Dr. Bob co-founded Alcoholics Anonymous with Bill Wilson in the 1930s.]

Like Bill W., Dr. Bob grew up in small-town New England. As an only child, he had religion forced on him early in life. It made him resolve never to set foot in a church after he grew up. He stuck with this for forty years except when he couldn't avoid it.

When Bob went to college, he drank like many other students, but he never got a hangover. Still he felt that he was an alcoholic from the start. He said, "My whole life seemed to be centered around doing what I wanted to do, without regard for the rights, wishes, or privileges of anyone else."

After working briefly, he began studying medicine. He drank huge amounts of beer in medical school and began getting the morning jitters for the first time. In his second year, he decided to leave school to live on a farm owned by a friend. When his brain cleared, he decided that quitting school was foolish. It took some talking to persuade his professors into taking him back.

A binge during exam week got him in trouble again, but he was allowed to finish school by promising not to touch another drop until graduation. He did so well that he won a prized internship in a Western hospital. There, he kept too busy to have time for drinking.

After graduation, he opened a private office. Stomach trouble sent him back to the bottle when he found that a couple of drinks relieved the pain. Soon he was at it again.

Dr. Bob put himself in treatment centers at least a dozen times, trying to control his alcohol use. Things went from bad to worse, until finally he was confined to bed for two months. Frightened by the experience, he abstained for a long spell.

Prohibition was in effect at the time, making liquor sales illegal in the U.S. When Dr. Bob learned that physicians were exempt from this law and could buy alcohol for medicinal purposes, he tried drinking in moderation. Before long, he was back to his old habits.

Most mornings, Dr. Bob didn't give in to his craving for alcohol. He had to, because when he drank, he couldn't work. Instead he took sedatives to calm his jitters. Over the next fifteen years, he had enough sense to avoid seeing patients while under the influence of liquor.

When his wife went out during the day, he'd smuggle bottles into the house and hide them in the coal bin, clothes chute, and cellar. He never used the water tank in the toilet because it seemed too obvious. He learned later that his wife often looked there. His bootlegger helped him hide fresh deliveries of alcohol.

He was so fearful of not sleeping that he got drunk every night, a habit that continued for seventeen years. Over and over, he promised his family he'd quit, but his promise seldom lasted through the day. His wife was afraid to invite friends over. They preferred to avoid him, anyway.

When beer became legal, he thought that was safe. With his wife's permission, he filled the cellar with cases of beer. Before long, he was drinking at least one and a half cases a day. He gained 30 pounds in two months and suffered shortness of breath.

One day, a woman called his wife and said she wanted Dr. Bob to meet a friend named Bill Wilson. Bill had conquered his obsession with alcohol using a spiritual approach, and she thought he might help Dr. Bob.

After a couple of talks with Bill, Dr. Bob stopped drinking for three weeks. But on the train to a medical conference in Atlantic City, he drank all the scotch in the bar car, continued his spree at the meeting, and drank all the way back. When he arrived home, his friends put him to bed and called his friend Bill. Bill brought him a few drinks to get him through the night and gave him a beer the next morning. That was June 10, 1935. Dr. Bob never drank after that.

Dr. Bob wrote that Bill W. was "the first living human with whom I had ever talked who knew what he was talking about in regard to alcoholism from actual experience. In other words, he talked my language."

Although it took Dr. Bob over two years to conquer his craving for liquor, he never came close to picking up another drink. His advice to alcoholics was, "If you still think you are strong enough to beat the game alone, that is your affair. But if you really and truly want to quit drinking liquor for good and all, and sincerely feel that you must have some help, we know that we have an answer for you. It never fails, if you go about it with one half the zeal you were in the habit of showing when you were getting another drink."

Made in the USA
Monee, IL
28 March 2022